A
Case for Charpentier

HISTORICAL PERFORMANCE
Dana Marsh

A
Case for Charpentier

TREATISE ON ACCOMPANIMENT AND COMPOSITION

TRANSLATED AND EDITED BY
CARLA E. WILLIAMS

INDIANA UNIVERSITY PRESS

This book is a publication of

Indiana University Press
Office of Scholarly Publishing
Herman B Wells Library 350
1320 East 10th Street
Bloomington, Indiana 47405 USA

iupress.org

Manufactured in the United States of America

Cataloging information is available from the Library of
Congress.

ISBN 978-0-253-05161-5 (hc)

First printing 2020

Contents

Acknowledgments

I am indebted to the Lilly Library of Indiana University, Bloomington, for making available the manuscript *Traité d'accompagnement* for translation and transcription and to the editors of Indiana University Press for seeing my edition into print.

Making a modern edition of an anonymous turn-of-the-eighteenth-century French treatise posed challenges related to notation, language, and theory. Numerous colleagues and scholars experienced in interpreting these and other issues, as well as those of the time and location, contributed valuable advice and encouragement. I am especially grateful to Kyle Adams, James Canary, the late Mary Wallace Davidson, Don Fader, David Lasocki, Daniel Melamed, Patricia Ranum, Graham Sadler, Joel Silver, Cherry Williams, and Elisabeth Wright for their generous support.

Special thanks are extended to Chris Renk and Joseph Walden for their skillful manipulation of the music notation software used in turning my transcription of a distinctive and frequently complex notation into a modern critical edition.

Translator's Introduction

Traité d'accompagnement (hereinafter *Traité*) is an anonymous, un-dated French manuscript that makes a valuable contribution to the existing literature on late seventeenth-century basse continue and music theory.[1] Its interest lies in its combined treatment of accompaniment and composition, its distinctive coverage of certain aspects of basse continue, and its placement in the theoretical continuum. Of special note is the identity of one of its authors.

The manuscript is written in two distinctly different hands, dividing it into two sections (hereinafter called Writer A and Charpentier—section A and section B). The first, that of Writer A, has yet to be identified. The second, found in a gathering of six leaves at the end of the manuscript, is similar in content and format to the *Règles de composition par Mr Charpentier* (H. 550) (hereinafter *Règles*), copied by Marc-Antoine Charpentier's colleague Etienne Loulié. The XLI written in the upper left corner of the first page of the gathering, folio 28r/f. 1r,[2] is akin to the numbering on the *cahiers* in Charpentier's *Meslanges autographes*. Indeed, in November 2009, Patricia Ranum recognized the writing on these leaves to be the hand of Charpentier. The identification was subsequently authenticated by two other Charpentier scholars, Catherine Cessac and Graham Sadler.[3] Table 1 contains a sampling of symbols, letters, and words found in the *Traité* in comparison with those found in the *Meslanges autographes*.

The table of contents found in the *Traité* divides it into two parts. In the first, Writer A addresses mode, meter, tempo, and the principles of basse continue. Part 2 begins with Writer A's discussion of dissonances and continues with "several curious essays."[4] These essays

---

1. *Traité d'accompagnement*, bound in with two other works, was acquired by the Lilly Library at Indiana University (call number MT530 .B73) from Bruce McKittrick Rare Books in 2000. The provenance before that date is unknown. For further information regarding the complete volume, see Physical Description below.

2. For an explanation of the foliation and pagination found in the *Traité*, see "Editorial Method and Physical Description," below.

3. Identification and authentication communicated through correspondence with this author.

4. *Traité*, f. 1v.

Table 1 Comparison of Charpentier's hand found in *Traité d'accompagnement* and in his *Meslanges autographes*.

	Traité d'accompagnement		Meslanges autographes	
Treble clef		G2 / f. 29r/f. 2r		G2 / Cahier LV, f. 9v
		G2 / f. 31v/f. 4v		G2 / Cahier LV, f. 1v
		G3 / f. 31v/f. 4v		G3 / Cahier 74, f. 24r
Bass clef		f. 28r/f. 1r		Cahier LV, f. 1r
C clef		C3 / f. 31r/f. 4r		C3 / Cahier LV, f. 25v
5		f. 32 r/f. 5r		Cahier LV, f. 16r
Sharp 4		f. 32 r/f. 5r		Cahier LV, f. 11v
Sharp 6		f. 29r/f. 2r		Cahier LV, f. 4r
Flat 6		f. 29r/f. 2r		Cahier LVIII, f. 28r

	Traité d'accompagnement		*Meslanges autographes*	
Capital P		f. 28r/f. 1r		Cahier LV, f. 25v
		f. 28v/f. 1v		Cahier LV, f. 6v
Capital T		f. 28r/f. 1r		Cahier LV, f. 6v
basse		f. 33v/f. 6v		Cahier LV, f. 22r
dessus		f. 28r/f. 1r		Cahier LV, f. 26v
flute		f. 33r/f. 6r		Cahier LX, f. 41r
troisieme		f. 33r/f. 6r		Cahier LX, f. 52v

Sources: Images in left column courtesy of the Lilly Library, Indiana University Bloomington. Images in right column courtesy of the Bibliothèque nationale de France.

are Charpentier's remarks regarding some aspects of basse continue, as well as a variety of compositional topics, including false relations, fugue, and parallel intervals.

Although the manuscript cannot be dated precisely, references found within place it around the turn of the eighteenth century. Writer A refers to the fifth edition of L'Affilard's *Principes très faciles pour bien apprendre la musique* (Paris, 1705), suggesting that the first portion was written after 1705.[5] We can assume that *Traité, ms. XLI* (what I use to refer to the six leaves in Charpentier's hand) was written before Charpentier's death in 1704, but it is possible to date it more precisely. Scholars have shown that the cahiers of the *Meslanges autographes* can be grouped together chronologically.[6] Specifically, Jane Gosine's extensive study of Charpentier's handwriting in the *Meslanges* shows that his clef formation changes over time. She describes three types of G and C clef signs (abbreviated as G-1, G-2, G-3, C-1, C-2, and C3) and categorizes them as early, middle, and late.[7] This analysis can also be used to date the *Traité, ms. XLI*. Table 1 shows examples of G-2, G-3, and C3 clefs found in the *Traité, ms. XLI* and compares them with those found in the *Meslanges*. In its entirety, there are five G-2, thirty-four G-3, and eight C-3 clefs (but no G-1, C-1, or C-2 clefs) present in the *Traité, ms. XLI*. Approximately seven of the G clefs appear to have begun as G-2s, as Patricia Ranum notes, but were amended to become G-3s.[8] The predominance of late G and C clefs, together with the dating of the later cahiers in the *Meslanges*, suggests that the *Traité, ms. XLI* dates from between 1685 and 1702.[9]

Until the discovery of the *Traité*, only one of Charpentier's surviving theoretical writings was in his own hand, his *Remarques sur les Messes à 16 parties d'Italie* (H. 549). The *Règles* and the *Abrégé des*

---

5. Ibid., f. 19v/p. 36.

6. See Shirley Thompson's comparison of dating methods in Shirley Thompson, "Reflections on Four Charpentier Chronologies," *Journal of Seventeenth-Century Music* 7, no. 1 (2001), accessed January 14, 2019, http://sscm-jscm.org/v7/no1/thompson.html.

7. C. Jane Gosine, "Questions of Chronology in Marc-Antoine Charpentier's Meslanges Autographes: An Examination of Handwriting Styles," *Journal of Seventeenth-Century Music* 12, no. 1 (2006), accessed January 14, 2019, https://sscm-jscm.org/v12/no1/gosine.html.

8. Ranum's thoughts concerning the dating of *Traité, ms. XLI* can be found on her website, Panat Times, accessed January 14, 2019, https://www.ranumspanat.com/.

9. See also Shirley Thompson, "Reflections on Four Charpentier Chronologies," *Journal of Seventeenth-Century Music* 7, no. 1 (2001), table 1, accessed January 14, 2019, http://sscm-jscm.org/v7/no1/thompson.html.

règles de l'accompagnement de Mʳ Charpentier (H. 551) exist only in the hand of Etienne Loulié.[10]

A comparison of Charpentier's remarks found in the *Traité, ms. XLI* and the *Règles* reveals a number of similarities and differences. The *Traité, ms. XLI* is generally less complete than the *Règles*; thoughts and explanations are comparatively abbreviated. Rather than a treatise prepared for publication, it resembles notes jotted down for a student during a lesson. Both treatises cover nearly the same topics: fugue, mode, meter, cadences, intervals, inversion, consonances, dissonances, diversity, imitation, modulation, false relations, and composition of a bass or treble part. Some of these subjects are similar in the way they are treated; others differ in the depth of coverage.

The initial pages of both sources are laid out in a like manner, beginning with a discussion of intervals—first, the perfect intervals of the octave, fifth, and fourth, followed by the imperfect intervals of major and minor thirds and sixths. Leading tones, both upper and lower, are considered soon after; the use of the sixth is given later in a separate section. Both the *Traité, ms. XLI* and the *Règles* emphasize the importance of including the third in every chord. The first words in the *Traité, ms. XLI* are "no harmony without a third." Near the beginning of the *Règles*, we read, "There is no harmony at all without the third."[11] This dictum is subsequently rephrased and repeated several more times in each source. Both discuss the sixth as an inversion of the third, but in the *Traité, ms. XLI*, Charpentier provides a charming analogy, comparing the beauty of a sixth to the reflection of a tree in the water.[12]

Dissonance is treated more simply in the *Traité, ms. XLI* than in the *Règles*. In the former, Charpentier gives general rules for the preparation and resolution of ninths, sevenths, fourths, and seconds, and he provides examples. The first mention of the subject in the *Règles* is a list of thirteen dissonances, which is followed by a discussion of their treatment.[13] Both sources clarify that although a fourth is a perfect consonance, it is sometimes considered a dissonance.[14]

In keeping with contemporaneous writers, Charpentier emphasizes the need to avoid parallel perfect intervals in both the *Traité, ms.*

---

10. Catherine Cessac, *Marc-Antoine Charpentier*, trans. E. Thomas Glasow (Portland, OR: Amadeus Press, 1995), 382.

11. *Traité*, f. 28r/f. 1r; Cessac, *Charpentier*, 389.

12. *Traité*, f. 32v/f. 5v.

13. *Traité*, f. 30r/f. 3r–f. 31r/f. 4r. Cessac, *Charpentier*, 398–404.

14. *Traité*, f. 30v/f. 3v; Cessac, *Charpentier*, 401.

XLI and the *Règles*, contrary motion being recommended as a way to avoid them. Less common is his assertion that several parallel fourths and fifths are acceptable, but only if they are of different types.[15] Parallel octaves are also allowable if they are between the parts. Charpentier stresses that although some parallel perfect intervals are permitted, two parallel octaves, "both accompanied by their third and by their fifth, are prohibited . . because these are two consecutive perfect consonances, which go against variety."[16]

Diversity is a recurring theme in both the *Traité, ms. XLI* and the *Règles*. The *Traité, ms. XLI* treats this theme in a more general, yet emphatic, way: "All that goes against variety is a great mistake in harmony."[17] The *Règles*, while not as forceful, identifies ways to create diversity, such as by avoiding parallel perfect intervals, using a variety of consonances and dissonances, and changing the tempo and mode.[18]

Compared with the *Règles*, certain topics are omitted from the *Traité, ms. XLI*. Consonances, for example, are touched on only when Charpentier states that the interval of a fourth can be either a consonance or a dissonance. Tempo, transposition, modulation, and key-feelings are not discussed. In contrast, the discussion of voice tessitura and its accompanying table that appear in the *Traité, ms. XLI* are not found in the *Règles*.

There are a number of striking similarities between the words of Writer A and Charpentier within the *Traité*. Writer A refers to Charpentier, even seeming to quote him at times. There is a marginal note on folio 10v: "Principles of Charpentier First Rule: No harmony without a third in several parts or against the bass." As already mentioned, in the *Traité, ms. XLI*, Charpentier writes, "No harmony without a third," and later, "Play a third against the bass or between the other parts, otherwise [there is] no harmony."[19] Another marginal note, this time referring to the sixth, is also similar to Charpentier's wording in the *Traité, ms. XLI*. On f. 10v (Writer A) we find, "II."[20] "The sixth against the bass or between the parts takes the place of the third," and on f. 28 r/f. 1r (Charpentier), also in a marginal note, we

15. *Traité*, f. 31v/f. 4v. Also see Cessac, Charpentier, 389–90.

16. *Traité*, f. 28v/f. 1v.

17. *Traité*, f. 28r/f. 1r.

18. See Cessac, *Charpentier*, 389, 392, 394, 397, 406.

19. *Traité*, f. 10v, f. 28r/f. 1r, f. 33v/f. 6v.

20. This "II" seems to refer to Charpentier's second rule.

read, "The sixth between the parts takes the place of the third."[21] In speaking of perfect intervals, Writer A states that they "allow neither augmentation nor diminution without being altered."[22] Charpentier writes that they "are called perfect because they permit neither augmentation nor diminution."[23] This familiarity with the teachings of Charpentier is accentuated when Writer A says, in reference to his statement that a consonant fourth can be played between the parts without preparation or resolution, that this was the "opinion of the late Charpentier."[24] In addition, Writer A recommends that beginners should play only thirds over the bass at first, later adding sixths and subsequently the other consonances. He admits that many composition treatises recommend this method but that he specifically took it from Charpentier and from Loulié.[25]

Accompaniment treatises from the decades around the turn of the eighteenth century often address similar issues. They commonly begin with the principles of music, such as notes and note values, intervals, and meter, before moving on to accompaniment. Basse continue topics often consist of range, part motion, chord inversion, and notes that can be included with those indicated by the figures. The *Traité* is unusual in comparison. Although Writer A does include some principles of music and of basse continue, he avoids discussion of other topics that he believes to have been well covered by other writers. For example, he informs us that figures show the distance between the bass and the note one must play, and he gives basic instruction for which notes to add to the chord. He does not write about intervals, however, because many books on composition and accompaniment provide material on the topic. He then refers the reader to the writings of Nivers and Masson for additional explanation.[26]

At other times, Writer A goes into more depth than is usual in comparison with other writers. One instance of this pertains to realizing an unfigured bass. As early as Bianciardi's *Breve regola* (1607), writers had presented guidelines for what to do when few or no figures are present with the bass line. These rules, which Campion termed the *rule of the octave* (1716), provided direction for realizing an unfigured bass according to certain characteristics of the bass

---

21. *Traité*, f. 10v, f. 28r/f. 1r.
22. *Traité*, f. 10v.
23. Ibid., f. 28r/f. 1r.
24. Ibid., f. 11v.
25. Ibid., f. 14v/p. 26.
26. Ibid., f. 3r, f. 7r.

line.[27] Writer A's guidelines for realizing an unfigured bass emphasize the importance of a thorough knowledge of the key and its chords, whether or not a bass line is figured. He writes that in the event that there are no figures, one should have "a perfect knowledge" of the fundamental chords and their progression in each key—and that it is necessary to know the mode well for manuscript music and in order to avoid being misled by printing errors.[28]

Writer A provides detailed directions regarding the accompaniment of dissonances. He explains that although he could have avoided speaking of them, since they are covered in many books, he chooses to goes into greater depth because other authors have been too brief or have not covered the topic clearly.[29]

His treatment of dissonances also differs at times from that of other writers. Saint Lambert, for example, says that a 2 can be accompanied with a doubled 5 or that the 2 can be doubled and accompanied by a 5. He specifies that this doubling is allowed when the bass descends a half step to a note that is not figured or that is figured with a 6. In this way, a third or its inversion, a sixth, is provided in the resolution. Writer A acknowledges this practice but does not deem it good, because it does not produce the interval of a third.[30]

A further example of Writer A's dissimilar treatment of dissonance is the addition of a 7 or a 9 to a chord. He instructs that a major or minor seventh can be added to a root-position chord without removing anything, although the octave may be removed if desired, whereas most writers say that you must have a 3 and should omit the 8 or the 5. Saint Lambert specifies that the 7 is better accompanied by the 3 and the 5, rather than with the 3 and the 8. Writer A says that the seventh and the ninth are often used together and that a major or minor ninth can be added by removing only the octave. In contrast, Saint Lambert instructs that a major ninth is accompanied with a 3 and a 5; a minor ninth, with a 3 and a 7.[31]

27. Francesco Bianciardi, *Breve regola para imparar'a sonare sul basso* (Siena, 1607). In *Œuvres théoriques completes*, Ars musices iuxta consignationes variorum scriptorium; Renaissance et période préclassique; Domaine Italien 1 (Paris: Editions du Cerf, 1996). François Campion, *Traité d'accompagnement et de composition selon la règle des octaves de musique; Addition au Traité d'accompagnement par la règle d'octave* (Paris, 1716; 1730; repr., Geneva: Minkoff, 1975).

28. *Traité*, f. 5r.

29. Ibid., f. 26v/p. 50–f. 27r, f. 25r/p. 47.

30. M. de Saint Lambert, *Nouveau traité de l'accompagnement du clavecin de l'orgue et des autres instruments* (Paris, 1707; repr., Geneva: Minkoff, 1972), 12; *Traité*, f. 26v/p. 50.

31. Saint Lambert, *Nouveau traité*, 16–17; *Traité*, f. 26v/p. 50.

The *petite sixte*, usually notated with a ♭6, 6♯, or even just 6, normally consists of 6/4/3. Writer A refers to this chord, saying that the sixth can be accompanied by a 4 or a tritone and a 3, but he also includes a less common chord, the "petite septième," presumably labeled with a 7. He describes it as being comprised of 8/7/3 or 8/7/5 in addition to the bass note.[32] Dandrieu also mentions a "Petite Sètième [*sic*]" but shows only examples of combining it with a 3 and an 8.[33]

Another unusual statement found in the *Traité* has to do with the placement of dissonance in triple meter. Before explaining dissonances, Writer A stresses the need to discuss meter and tempo, reasoning that without an understanding of them, one will not know where to place the dissonances properly. He differentiates between duple and triple meters in the placement of dissonance. In duple meter, dissonances must be prepared on a weak beat, played on a strong beat, and resolved on a weak beat. Although nothing is said about preparation or resolution of dissonance in triple meter, Writer A specifies that one can place dissonances on any of the three beats.[34] As accents do occur in triple-meter French music and are normally found on beat one, beat two, or both beats, Writer A's statement may refer to occasions when the usually weak third beat is used as a dramatic upbeat, an entire measure is an upbeat, or there is a hemiola from one measure to the next.

The *Traité* as a whole is indicative of a time when music theory was in flux, moving from modality to tonality. Prominent in this change was a decrease from multiple modes to only two, major and minor, affecting the way the term *transposition* was understood. Contemporaneous treatises and performance manuals highlight these changes.

In his *Méthode claire, certaine et facile pour apprendre à chanter la musique* (Paris, 1691), Jean Rousseau teaches how to "naturalize" transposed modes. He lists the modes that are transposed by B-flat and B-natural, making a distinction between those with a major third and those with a minor third. To be able to sing in all the modes, one must naturalize them by placing ut on a different note and by becoming acquainted with the locations of the two semitones (mi to fa; si to ut). One imagines a different clef, paying attention to where the

---

32. *Traité*, f. 27r.

33. Jean-François Dandrieu, *Principes de l'accompagnement du clavecin* (Paris, 1719; repr., Geneva: Minkoff, 1972), 34.

34. *Traité*, f. 19r/p. 35, f. 27r.

two semitones should fall, in order to treat the transposed modes as if they are natural.[35]

Etienne Loulié also differentiates between natural and transposed music in *Eléments ou principes de musique* (Paris, 1696). He explains that natural music is that which has no sharps or flats in the key signature, whereas transposed music has one or more. His explanation of transposition is relatively simple: one should detach the *ut* from the letter *C* and put it with another letter, transferring the semitones from where they are in the natural mode to the transposed mode. In other words, *ut* can be placed on any note.[36]

Through his treatment of the foregoing principles, Writer A also embraces aspects of emerging tonality but has not discarded modality. He refers to the past, when there had been several modes, affirming that there are now only two—major and minor—which are modeled on C ut (C major) and D ut (D minor). He explains that most people consider transposed music to be that which is written in different keys, with different key signatures. His opinion is that this practice is "to play it in its natural order"—that transposition is actually when one plays the music higher or lower than it is written; one must imagine another key.[37]

Writer A's explanation of why he does not give notes their "ordinary names" is related to this. He refers to Loulié's philosophy that *ut* can be placed on all the notes of the scale by means of sharps and flats. Because of this, he believes it is unnecessary to use three solmization syllables to name a note. He points out that, although this practice was logical in plainchant, it is now pointless and there is "room to hope" that people will instead use only two (e.g., C ut instead of C sol ut).[38]

Physical Description

The *Traité* is bound in with two other works, Pierre Borjon de Scellery's *Traité de la mvsette: avec vne novvelle methode, pour*

---

35. Jean Rousseau, *Méthode claire, certaine et facile pour apprendre à chanter la musique* (Paris, 1691), 21–23; trans. Robert A. Green as *A Clear, Sure, and Easy Method for Learning to Sing* in his "Annotated Translation and Commentary of the Works of Jean Rousseau: A Study of Late Seventeenth-Century Musical Thought and Performance Practice" (PhD diss., Indiana University, 1979), 21–23, 203–5.

36. Etienne Loulié, *Eléments ou principes de musique* (Paris, 1696); trans. Albert Cohen (New York: Institute of Mediaeval Music, 1965), 22.

37. *Traité*, f. 6r, f. 8r–f. 8v.

38. Ibid, f. 7v–f. 8r.

apprendre de soy-mesme à joüer de cét instrument facilement, & en peu de temps (Lyon, 1672) and an anonymous satirical play entitled *Au Loup*. The composite volume measures 33 centimeters high by 22 centimeters wide by 3 centimeters thick. It is calf covered and sprinkled with copperas (ferrous sulfate); all edges have designs tooled in gold. The full-gilt spine is sewn on five raised bands, with end bands of blue and white silk, and is lined with paper or parchment. There are small repairs to the head and tail of the spine. Spine linings are visible on paste-down endpapers, and fragments of manuscript waste can be seen underneath.

The foxing on the endpapers and the adjacent leaves matches, indicating a binding contemporaneous with the writings within. Although split in places, the endpapers are conjugate leaves, with threads visible, and a watermark appears on the front free endpaper and the back paste-down endpaper. The endpapers are relatively free of marking, with the exception of an inscription in the front and some erasures in the back.[39] The inscription "Lepres Levayer" is in ink in the upper right-hand corner of the front paste-down endpaper. The text block measures 32.3 centimeters high by 21 centimeters wide by 2 centimeters thick, and its edges are sprinkled with red dye.

The first of three items bound into the volume, the anonymous undated manuscript *Traité d'accompagnement*, consists of thirty-three leaves. Modern penciled foliation is found throughout the entire manuscript in the upper right-hand corners. As already mentioned, the *Traité* is written in two different hands, dividing it into two sections. Section A consists of folios 1 through 27. The leaves of this section are much the same size as the text block as a whole, although a number of them are somewhat larger than the rest, apparently a result of marginal notes or the addition of staff paper, and have been folded in such a way as to fit within the dimensions of the text block. The staves of the musical examples and of the occasional leaves of staff paper appear to be drawn with rastra. Beginning with folio 13r, contemporaneous ink pagination has been added to the upper fore-edge corners, starting with the numeral 23 and continuing through 50. Folios 23 through 25 are trimmed in such a way that only fragments of numerals 43 through 48 are visible. Numerals 1 through 22, 51, and 52 may have been present but were then subsequently cropped

39. Attempts to ascertain what was erased have been unsuccessful thus far, but it may be a bookseller's price code.

Figure 1. Watermarks found in section A.

completely at binding. Catchwords appear inconsistently throughout section A.

Section B consists of folios 28 through 33 and was foliated contemporaneously in ink with the numerals 1 through 6. This section is written entirely on staff paper, both text and examples. There are twelve staves per page; the groupings of staves, minus page margins, measure 20.9 centimeters high by 14.5 centimeters wide. The staff lines appear to have been made with rastra, with some extensions drawn in by hand. The paper of section B is smaller than the text block as a whole, measuring approximately 29 centimeters high by 16.5 centimeters wide. It is darker than the paper in section A, and the edges are somewhat uneven. Strips of lighter-colored paper have been glued to the edges, extending the size of the leaves to be equal to that of the text block. A patch is present on folio 30v, but what is

Figure 2. Collation of the *Traité*, as seen from the tail. Section A is shown by the top three gatherings; section B, by the bottom two.

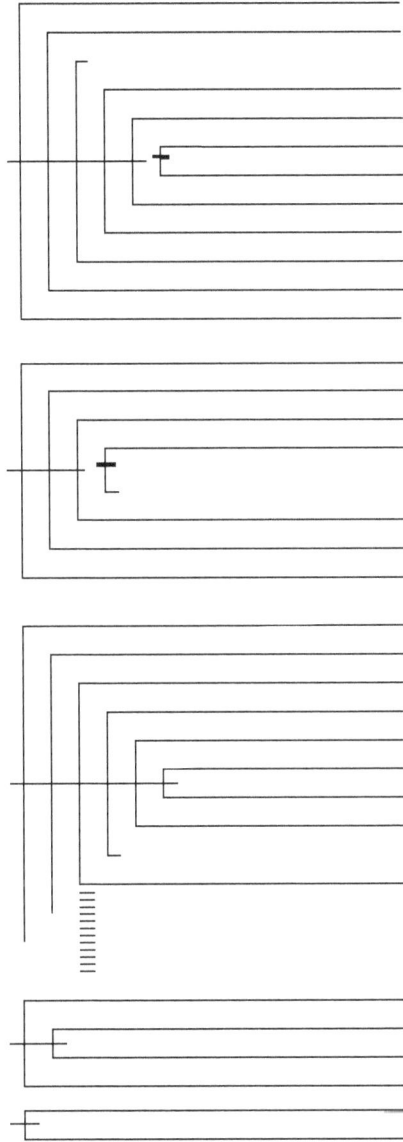

underneath it is not visible. All six leaves appear to have been folded together horizontally across the middle, probably with rectos in, as the outer page (folio 33v) is dirtier than the rest. Three lines of text on folio 33v are written in lighter ink than that of the rest of the section. These look as though they are in a third hand. In addition, the clef signs found in example 39 on folio 33v are not written in the same way as those of either Writer A or Charpentier. Both the example and

its explanation are squeezed in between the text and the word "Fin." Six watermarks are present throughout section A; none are found in section B.

The complicated collation is necessarily conjectural, to some extent, because of the tightness of the binding. Stubs are present, and there is a variety of paper. In addition to regular sewing, two places have an attachment in darker thread (indicated in bold in fig.2). Folds in section B are obscured by the binding.

The second of the three items in the binding is Pierre Borjon de Scellery's *Traité de la mvsette* (Lyon, 1672). The third and final item is a satirical play titled *Au Loup*. A dedication to "Monseigneur" by "votre fille Helaine" is found on folio 1v through folio 2r. At the bottom of folio 2r is written "Quant Octobre prend sa fin la Tousaint est au matin 1695," suggesting a date of October 31, 1695.

Editorial Method

Every attempt has been made to transcribe the manuscript with care and precision and to achieve a proper balance between a word-for-word translation and one so free that the original sense is lost.

Text

Paragraphs in the manuscript are indicated with extra spacing between lines, sometimes indented and sometimes not. In both transcription and translation, each paragraph has been indented. Long, convoluted sentences have been broken up and archaic punctuation modernized in order to provide clarity. In the manuscript, abbreviations occur both midword and at the ends of words. Some are characterized by one missing letter or more and a curved line above the adjacent vowel, whereas others have one missing letter or more followed by a superscripted final letter. Abbreviated words have been transcribed by including the missing letter(s) in italics (e.g., "gra*n*de," "musi*que*," "accompagnm*en*ᵗ"). These words have not been abbreviated in the translation. Some missing letters are a result of tight binding, trimmed edges, or author error; these are supplied in square brackets in the transcription. Words that were heavily marked out in the manuscript are not included in the transcription if they appear to be the same as what follows. Words with a single line drawn through them and followed by a different word are, however, included in the

transcription. Words or phrases are grouped together with brackets in several locations in the manuscript, sometimes including explanations for the groupings. The bracketed items have been separated by slashes in the transcription; in the translation, they have been formed into sentences. Catchwords, found on nearly every page of section A, were omitted in both the transcription and the translation. Extraneous marks, such as the lines separating items in the table of contents, have been left out. Foliation and pagination often appear together in the *Traité*; the transcription and the translation retain both (e.g., f. 26v/p. 50, or f. 30r/f. 3r).[40]

Musical Examples

English translations appear in brackets adjacent to the French text. C clefs and French violin clefs have been changed to treble clefs in order to make the examples more accessible to the modern reader. Although stem direction is as faithful to the manuscript as possible, it was not feasible to recreate exactly which side of the note the stem is on. Sharp and flat symbols meant to cancel previous accidentals have been entered as natural signs, except for example G, f. 4r, which is an explanation of how the French and Italians do this differently. In section A of the manuscript, examples are often labeled internally with uppercase letters. The letters are not always unique; Writer A reuses them for subsequent examples. A bracketed label has been added below each example for easier identification. Folio numbers have been added to those marked with uppercase letters in the original (e.g., [example A, f. 3v]). Those without labels in the manuscript have been assigned lowercase letters (in section A) or numerals (in section B), also followed by folio numbers (e.g., [example a, f. 3v]; [example 1, f. 28r/f. 1r]).

Terminology Choices

Accord *(Chord; Interval)*

French theorists writing around 1700 normally are in agreement with Saint Lambert's definition of *accord* as "a production

---

40. For further detail concerning foliation and pagination in the *Traité*, see "Physical Description," above.

of several sounds at once, which forms an agreeable consonance."[41] In the *Traité*, Writer A uses the word *accord* when describing both chords and intervals. In explaining that a third, a fifth, or an octave should be played on an unfigured bass note, he states that "these three notes will form the perfect chord" (*accord*).[42] Later, he remarks on the rarity of the interval (*accord*) of the diminished fourth.[43] Consequently, *accord* has been translated according to context, with *chord* referring to the playing of several notes together and *interval* referring to the distance between two notes.

Choque la diversité
(Offend variety; go against variety)

This somewhat cryptic phrase emphasizes the importance of variety in accompaniment: that a lack of variety is an offense. Charpentier uses these words several times in section B in reference to parallel perfect intervals. The first instance emphasizes that parallel fifths are monotonous and are to be avoided: "All that goes against variety is a great mistake in harmony. That is why two consecutive fifths of the same type are forbidden."[44]

Corde *(Note)*

Writer A uses the terms *corde* and *notte* when referring to notes. In an accompaniment treatise for a harpsichord, it seems sensible to translate *corde* as "note" rather than "string." Indeed, Brossard defines *corde* as "not only the strings of an instrument, but all the notes or delicate sounds which are contained in the span of the octave or range. Thus one says note A, note B, to express the sound A mi la, B fa si, etc."[45]

---

41. "Un Accord est une production de plusieurs sons tout à la fois, lesquels forment par leur assemblage une Consonnance agreeable," M. de Saint Lambert, *Les principes du clavecin* (Paris, 1702; repr., Geneva: Minkoff Reprints, 1972), 64.

42. *Traité*, f. 3v.

43. Ibid., f. 26r/p. 49.

44. "Tout ce qui choque la diversité est une grande faute en har[m]onie. C'est pourquoy deux quintes de semblable espece de suite sont deffendues," *Traité*, f. 28r/f. 1r.

45. "Veut dire CORDE & signifie non seulement les cordes d'un Instrument, mais toutes les *Nottes* ou *Sons sensibles* qui sont renfermez dans l'étenduë de l'Octave ou *Diapson*. ainsi on dit *la Corde A*. la Corde *B*. &c. pour exprimer le Son d'A, *mi, la*, de B, *fa, si, &c,*" Sebastien de Brossard, *Dictionnaire de musique*,

Faux *(False)*

Altered; dissonant.

Juste *(Perfect)*

Unaltered; true to the scale.

Mode *(Mode)*

In the 1690s, Loulié, Masson, and others use the terms *mode* and *ton* synonymously, writing of *mode majeure* and *mode mineure*.[46] Writer A asserts that this meaning of *ton* is incorrect, although usage dictates otherwise (see "Ton," below). Within the *Traité*, both *mode* and *ton* are used when referring to key. To avoid adding confusion, *mode* has been translated as "mode" and *ton* as "key."

Modulation *(Modulation)*

Contrary to the modern sense of moving from one key to another, *modulation* in early eighteenth-century France referred to the movement from one note or chord to another. The *Dictionnaire de l'Académie française* (1694) defines *modulation* as a "song which moves from one sound to another, according to certain notes or consonances that are pleasing to the ear."[47]

Mouvement *(Tempo)*

According to Brossard, the word *mouvement* "sometimes simply means the passage from one sound to another sound" or "sometimes it indicates the slowness or the quickness of the notes

contenant une explication des termes Grecs, Latins, Italiens, & François, les plus usitez das la musique, 2nd ed. (Paris, 1705; repr., Hilversum, Netherlands: Frits Knuf, 1965), 16.

46. Loulié, *Eléments ou principes de musique*, 65–66; Charles Masson, *Nouveau traité des règles pour la composition de la musique* (Paris, 1699, repr., New York: Da Capo Press, 1967), 9–12.

47. "Modulation. s.f. Chant qui varie d'un son à autre, suivant certaines notes ou consonances agreables à l'oreille. *La modulation de cette basse est fort belle*," *Dictionnaire de l'Académie française*, 1st ed. (1694); in the ARTFL Project, accessed September 1, 2011, http://artfl-project.uchicago.edu/content/dictionnaires-dautrefois.

and the meter, thus one says happy tempo, slow tempo, quick tempo, or animated."[48] In the *Traité*, *mouvement* refers to tempo.

Supposition *(Substitution)*

To use a dissonance in place of a consonance, French Baroque composers use several types of dissonances in conjunction with the term *supposition*. Charpentier provides an example of a suspension, explaining "that the fourth resolved into a third is only a substitution (*supposition*) or a suspension of the third."[49] In the first edition of *Traité d'accompagnement pour le théorbe et le clavecin*, Delair describes passing tones when defining *supposition*,[50] while in his *Nouveau traité d'accompagnement pour le theorbe, et le clavessin* he refers to dissonant chords that take the place of consonant ones—specifically delineating that the fourth takes the place of the third, the sixth takes the place of the fifth, and the seventh and the ninth take the place of the octave.[51]

Syncoper *(Syncopate)*

Referring to the introduction of a dissonance by means of a preparation and a resolution.

Ton *(Key; Tone)*

Loulié lists three ways in which the term *ton* is used: (1) the distance from one sound to another—interval; (2) mode—key;

---

48. "Ce terme a plusieurs significations différentes dans la Musique. Quelque fois il signifie simplement le passage d'un Son à un autre Son. . . . Quelques fois il signifie la *Lenteur*, ou la *Vitesse* des Nottes & de la mesure, ainsi on dit, mouvement *gay*, mouvement *lent*, mouvement *vif*, ou *animé*, &c. & dans ce sens il signifie aussi souvent une *égalité*, *reglée* & bien *marquée* de tous les temps de la mesure. C'est en ce sens qu'on dit que le *Recitatif* ne se chante pas de *mouvement*; que le *Menuet*, la *Gavotte*, la *Sarabande*, &c. sont des airs de *mouvement*, &c," Brossard, *Dictionnaire de musique*, 56.

49. "Ce dernier exemple montre que la quarte sauvee en tierce n'est qu'une supposition ou une suspension de la tierce," *Traité*, f. 28r/f. 1r.

50. Denis Delair, *Traité d'accompagnement pour le théorbe et le clavecin* (Paris, 1690; repr., Geneva: Minkoff, 1972), 60–61.

51. Denis Delair, *Nouveau traité d'accompagnement pour le theorbe, et le clavessin* (Paris, 1724; reprint in *Basse continue: France 1600–1800: Methodes, traites, ouvrages generaux, prefaces, periodiques*, v. 2, [réalisés] by Jean Saint-Arroman, 145–94. Courlay: Editions Fuzeau, 2006), 154.

and (3) a degree of determined sound—pitch.[52] The ambiguity of the term is underscored by Writer A, who says, "One also calls mode '*ton*,' but this is most improper, since the word *ton* is only intended to express the distance from one sound to another, as in Ut to Re, Sol to La, etc. However, it is necessary to acknowledge that usage has decided it completely differently, and one says equally today that a piece is composed, for example, in the *mode* or *ton* of C sol ut or D la re, etc."[53] In the *Traité*, *ton* is also used in terminology referring to scale degrees: *Demiton favori*; *Semiton favori*; *Semiton sensible*; *Semiton sensitive*; and *Ton favori* (leading tone).

---

52. "Le mot de *Ton* a plusieurs Significations. 10. *Ton signifie une certain distance ou intervalle d'un Son à un autre Son, comme* d'*Ut* à *Re*. 20. *Ton signifie ce* que les Musiciens appellant Mode. . . . 30. *Ton* signifie un Degré de Son determine," Etienne Loulié, *Eléments ou principes de musique, mis dans un nouvel ordre* (Paris, 1696, repr., Geneva: Minkoff, 1971), 77.

53. *Traité*, f. 5v.

Traité d'accompagnement

Parallel Transcription
and Translation

[Marginal note: 13. au. 26.

30 [ ] [ ]]

TREATISE ON
ACCOMPANIMENT

Table of Contents

[Marginal note: 13. au. 26.

30 [ ] Deffend.[1]]

Ly[2]
TRAITÉ
D'ACCOMPAG
NEMENT

Table

---

1. This note is difficult to decipher. The second line suggests a price, as it begins with what appears to be "30" and is followed by what may be an "l." It is uncertain what the final word is or means.

2. This looks like the letters "L" and "y," but the meaning is unclear. Partially written over the word "*Traité*," the letters are probably not a part of the title.

3. We might expect to see "*quarte consonante*" here instead of "*quarte consonance;*" indeed Writer A uses the former term on f. 14r/p. 25. Nonetheless, "*consonance*" appears here and in several other places (e.g., f. 11v) when referring to the same phenonenon.

f. 2r

[blank]

f. 2v

Treatise on Accompaniment
and Composition
Foreword

Accompaniment on the harpsichord depends a great deal on some ideas from composition, and the harpsichord is so convenient for imparting a perfect understanding of the arrangement of the voices above each other; that it should not be surprising if I speak of [accompaniment and composition] in general without distinction.

I will begin with the elements of composition. I think, in this regard, that there is no precise rule for producing on one's own a treble or bass melody, which is what is called composing a subject. That depends on the taste of the composer, and I think that one need not give examples of it. Taste is formed with time through the practice of good music, which is often scarcely acquired [even] after many years. It is therefore necessary at first, without diverting oneself by composing a treble or a bass, which can only be very irregular and very bad, to take a bass for a subject from [the works] of good composers such as Lully, Corelli, Bernier, etc., and to study composing one upper part, and several months later, several [parts], according to the progress one makes. The harpsichord is excellent for advancing this study, in that it readily shows all the chords that can

f. 3r

be played on a bass note.

The reason it is necessary to begin by taking a bass for one's subject, and not a treble for making a bass, is that the bass is the foundation of the harmony, and that the intervals derive their names only from their distance from the bass. Thus, the third is called third only because it is raised three degrees above the bass, and thus for all the other consonances and dissonances. In a word, the bass is in music what the foundation of a house is in architecture.

f. 2r

[blank]

f. 2v

**Traité D'accompagnement
et de composition
Avant propos**

L'accompagnement du clavecin depend beaucoup de quelques idées de composition, et le clavecin est si commode pour donner l'intelligence parfaite de l'arrangement des parties les unes au dessus des autres, qu'il ne faut pas s'estonner si je parle en general de l'un et de l'autre, sans distinction.

Je commenceray par les elemens de composition, et je pense a cet egard, qu'il n'y a aucune regle precise pour produire de soy mesme un chant de dessus, ou de basse, qui est ce que l'on appelle former un sujet. cela depend du goust d'un compositeur, et je croy qu'on ne doit point en donner des exemples. Le goust se forme avec le temps dans la pratique de la bonne musique, ce qui est souvent a peine le fruit de plusieurs années: Il faut donc d'abord, sans s'amuser a composer de soy mesme un dessus, ou une basse, qui ne peuvent estre, que tres Irreguliers, et tres mauvais, prendre une basse pour son sujet, dans de bons autheurs comme Lully, Corelli, Bernier &c, et s'estudier a composer dessus, une partie, et quelques mois apres, plusieurs, selon le progres, que l'on fera. Le clavecin est excellent pour avancer dans cette estude, en ce qu'il montre en un moment, tous les accords, qui se peuvent

f. 3r

pratiquer sur une notte de basse.

La raison, pour la quelle il faut commencer par prendre une basse pour son sujet, et non pas un dessus pour y faire une basse, est, que la basse est le fondement de l'harmonie, et que les accords ne tirent leur nom, que de la distance, qu'ils ont de la basse: Ainsy la tierce ne s'apelle tierce, que parce qu'elle est elevée de trois degres au dessus de la basse, et ainsy de toutes les autres consonances et dissonances; En un mot, la basse est dans la musique, ce que sont les fondemens d'une maison dans l'architecture.

One can judge by that how important it is to choose a well-constructed subject for making a good treble. The composers I have just named are excellent for that. Their harmony is piquant. That of Lully is the simplest and the easiest for beginners; but that of Corelli is mellower and more regular. Thus I would recommend working on the adagios by this composer.

Before going into further detail, it is necessary to point out that it is easy to write a treble or to accompany slow movements when the basses are well figured, since the figures show the distance the interval is from the bass or the note one must play. An example will make this understandable.

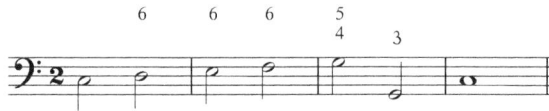

[Example a, f. 3v]

This example shows that a beginner, without straining the imagination to produce a melody, can write the treble as the figures indicate, which would produce [example] A.

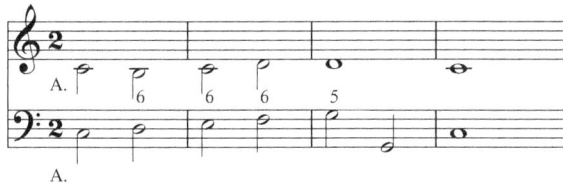

[Example A, f. 3v]

or simply with the third, [example] B.[1]

[Example B, f. 3v]

---

1. In other words, you can produce a treble line by following the interval above the bass, whether marked as 6 or implied as 3.

On peut juger par la, de quelle importance il est de choisir un sujet bien conduit pour faire un bon dessus. Les autheurs, que je viens de nommer excellent pour cela, Leur harmonie est pleine de sel celle de Lully est la plus simple, et la plus aisée pour les commence-mens; mais celle de Corelli est plus moileuse, et plus reguliere: ainsy je conseillerois de travailler sur Des Adagio de cet autheur;

Avant d'entrer dans un detail plus long, il faut remarquer, qu'il est aisé d'ecrire un dessus, ou d'accompagner, les mouvemens lens quand les basses sont bien chiffrées, puisque les chiffres font voir a quelle distance de la basse est l'accord, ou la corde qu'on doit toucher. Un exemple fera comprendre cecy.

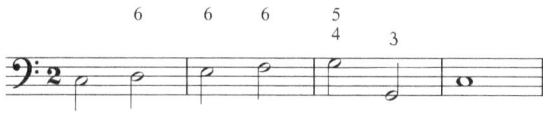

[Example a, f. 3v]

Cet Exemple fait connoistre, qu'un commençant, sans forcer son imagination, pour produire un chant, peut Ecrire le dessus comme les chiffres le marquent: ce qui produiroit. A

[Example A, f. 3v]

ou bien a la tierce simplement B.

[Example B, f. 3v]

When there is nothing indicated above a bass note, it is always a third, a fifth, or an octave that one must write, or play on the harpsichord if one accompanies. These three notes form the perfect chord, which will be discussed later. I do not give an example of this last rule. The example which I have just given must serve [for that purpose].

When there is also only a sharp (♯), a natural (♮), or a flat (♭) over the bass note, without a number beside it, that is always understood to determine the third that is played on this bass. Thus, the flat, [example] C, shows

[Examples C and D, f. 3v]

that in the chord of G sol, the third, which is B, must be minor, and the sharp, [example] D, shows that in the chord of A la, the third, which is C ut, must be major at the approach to the final cadence. These two notes are essential in the minor mode. I will explain the reason for that elsewhere. It is enough for the present to point out that by means of the flat, one changes the third of the bass from major to minor, as it was before, [example] E,

f. 4r

and by means of the sharp or the natural, on the contrary, one changes the third of the bass from minor to major, as it was before, [example] F.

[Example E, f. 4r]

Quand il n'y a rien de marqué au dessus d'une note de basse, c'est toujours une tierce, une quinte, ou une octave, qu'il faut ecrire; ou toucher sur le clavecin, si l'on accompagne: ces trois cordes forment l'accord parfait, dont il sera parlé dans la suite: Je ne donne point de demonstration de cette derniere regle: l'exemple, que je viens de donner en doit servir.

Quand il n'y a aussy sur la note de basse, qu'un dieze, ♯ ou un ♮. quarre, ou un b. mol, sans chiffre a costé, cela s'entend toujours pour determiner la tierce, qui se joüe sur cette basse. Ainsy le b. mol C. fait voir,

[Examples C and D, f. 3v]

que dans l'accord de la notte G. sol, la tierce, qui est B. Si doit estre mineure, et le diese D. fait voir, que dans l'accord de la notte A la, la Tierce, qui est C. ut doit estre majeure, pour tomber a la cadence finale:

Ces deux notes sont essentielles au mode mineur: j'en expliqueray la raison ailleurs. Il suffit, presentement, de faire remarquer, que par le moyen du b mol, on rend la tierce de la basse, mineure, de majeure, qu'elle estoit, E

f. 4r

et que par le moyen du dieze ou du ♮. quarre, on rend au contraire la tierce de la basse, majeure, de mineure, qu'elle estoit F.

[Example E, f. 4r]

[Example F, f. 4r]

In French music, the natural serves only to raise [a note by] a semitone, like the sharp, as has just been explained. But in the [works of] Italian composers, it often serves to lower [a note], when a note on which the sharp is found returns to the normal modulation,[2] by removing the sharp, [example] G.

[Example G, f. 4r]

By "normal modulation," I mean the diatonic modulation of an octave, without flats and sharps. The natural is used, therefore, in all the transposed keys, such as B [minor], F-sharp minor, and others. The reason is plain: because the natural is used only to restore to nature the note on which it is placed by lowering a sharped note into the diatonic order, just as it returns the B si- and E mi-flats when they ascend. This [practice] is not, however, without opponents, but this is not the place for an essay [on this subject]. It is enough to warn that this manner of lowering sharped notes with a natural is common in Italian music, which sometimes confuses beginners, since our masters use the natural only to raise [notes]

---

2. See *modulation* in "Terminology Choices," located in the introduction.

[Example F, f. 4r]

Dans la musique françoise le ♮. ne sert, que pour hausser de semiton, comme le dieze, ainsy, qu'il vient d'estre expliqué, mais dans
les autheurs italiens, il sert souvent a baisser, quand une notte, sur la
quelle le diese se trouve, rentre dans la modulation ordinaire en ostant le dieze G.

Comme s'il y avoit [as if there were]

G. re sol maj.   G   G
[G major]

[Example G, f. 4r]

J'entens par la modulation ordinaire, la modulation diatonique de
l'octave, qui est sans b mol et sans diezes: Le ♮. se pratique donc dans
tous les Tons transposez, comme b. si ♮. F. fa diezé mi. & autres: La
raison est naturelle; le ♮. n'estant fait, que pour remettre en nature la
notte, sur la quelle on le met, il fait rentrer en baissant une notte diesée
dans l'ordre diatonique, comme il y fait rentrer les B. Si, et les E mi b
mols, quand il les fait monter. Cecy n'est pourtant pas sans contradic-
teurs, mais ce n'est pas icy le lieu d'une dissertation: Il suffit d'avertir
que cette maniere de baisser les notes diesées par un ♮. est commune
dans la musique Italienne, ce qui trompe quelques fois les commençans; a cause, que nos maistres n'employent le ♮. que pour monter de

by a semitone. Even their [the Italians'] books do not discuss it differently. There is still another way to use the natural which is common to all composers. When the modulation of a key that one is using seems to lead to another whose nature is ambiguous, one precedes this note with a [natural sign] to signify that it must be played naturally, or in a word, in nature [example] H.[3]

[Example H, f. 4v]

This example is drawn from Corelli's Op. 3, No. 9, in F minor, where one sees a natural (♮) on G sol and D re, [example] H to warn that the G sol is not flat, although the modulation might demand it, and that D re, which in this key is ordinarily flat because it is the sixth, and that any sixth of a minor mode is minor as we will show elsewhere; that D re is, as I say, without a flat, as the key signature conveys.

Another general principle is that on all natural semitones, such as Si to Ut and Mi to Fa, and transposed ones, such as Ut-sharp to Re, Fa-sharp to Sol, and Sol-sharp to La, the sixth is always good in composition and in accompaniment; ordinarily it is figured thus [6], [example] I.

[Example I, f. 4v]

All the other intervals are ordinarily figured with precision in printed music. But to

---

3. This example is mm. 29–36 of the Largo in Corelli's Op. 3, No. 9. There are figures present in the score, but presumably Writer A did not wish to create confusion by including them while discussing accidentals. The various editions show the first note of the second measure as a C-natural instead of a G-natural. Opus 3 was first published in 1689 in Rome by Giacomo Komarek and in Paris ca. 1718 by H. Foucault.

de [*sic*] semiton: Leurs Livres mesmes n'en parlent pas autrement. Il y a encor une maniere d'employer le ♮., qui est commune a tous les autheurs: Quand la modulation Du Ton, que l'on traite semble porter a une notte, dont la corde est douteuse, on precede cette notte d'un ♮. pour exprimer, qu'il la faut toucher naturelleme*n*ᵗ comme elle est, ou en un mot, En nature, H.

[Example H, f. 4v]

Cette exemple est tiré du troisieme œuvre de corelli, Sonate neuf. En F. fa tierce mineure; ou l'on voit un ♮. sur un G. Sol H, et sur un D Re H, pour advertir que ce G. Sol n'est pas b. mol, quoyque la modulation le pûst demander, et que D. Re, qui dans ce ton est ordinairement b. mol, parce qu'il en est la sixte, et que toute sixte de Mode mineur, est mineure, comme nous le montrerons ailleurs; que D Re, dis je, est sans b mol, comme la clef le porte.

Un autre principe general, c'est que sur tous les semito*n*s naturels, comme du Si a l'ut, et du Mi au fa, et transposez, comme de l'ut diezé au re, du fa diezé au Sol, et du Sol diezé au la, la sixte y est toujours bonne dans la composition, et dans l'accompagnement: ordinairement elle y est chiffrée: ainsy. .I.

[Example I, f. 4v]

Tous les autres accords sont chiffrez ordinairement avec exactitude dans les musiques imprimées: Mais, pour

f. 5r

avoid being misled by printing errors, which are often found, and for playing manuscript music, which is often not figured at all, it is necessary to know well the mode in which a piece is composed. A perfect knowledge of the modulation of the [basic] chords or essentials of each key, together with a little practice, avoids all confusion. Such modulation will be discussed in the first section of this treatise.[4] Without this knowledge, it is very difficult to determine by oneself whether the thirds are major or minor, when a bass is not figured. Sixths are even more difficult [to determine], unless knowledge is supplemented with a great deal of practice and a bit of good taste. I assume that in order to understand all these things, one has some inkling of vocal music, because without these rudiments many things would be unintelligible. I also assume one knows that all the parts except the bass are played by the right hand.[5] The surest thing is to have a good teacher, without whom it is very difficult to learn other than by time and patience. Books are not without their use for that. They serve to encourage the student to ask the teacher questions, and from that to gather instructions which strengthen the ideas that speculation gives about the first principles.

f. 5v

On Mode and of Its Essential Notes

There are some authors who discuss the differences between chords, but I have not seen any of them say precisely the reason why one sharpens or flattens certain notes in the most standard vocal modulation and in instrumental music. However, that which appears to me so necessary to know in order to compose and to accompany accurately, that one cannot acquire without long study or even longer practice. The following rules will show with certainty the reason for the diversity of harmony on bass notes which seem to be the same. One modern author defines mode as a way to begin and to direct a melody by the notes which are related naturally to a certain note and to conclude it with the same note, which is called the final.

---

4. See f. 5v.

5. There are differences of opinion regarding this. Some (e.g., Corrette and Dandrieu) agree with Writer A; others (e.g., d'Anglebert, Saint Lambert, and Nivers) maintain that the accompaniment can be shared by both hands.

f. 5r

n'estre point trompé par les fautes d'impression, qui se trouvent souvent, et pour joüer la musique a la main, qui souvent n'est point du tout chiffrée; Il faut bien connoistre le mode, dans lequel une piece est composée: La parfaite connoisance de la Modulation des cordes favorites, ou essentielles de chaque Ton, avec un peu de pratique oste tout embarras; c'est de cette modulation dont il sera parlé dans la Premiere division de ce traité; sans la connoistre il est bien difficile de Determiner de soy mesme la nature des Tierces, pour les faire majeures, ou mineures, quand une basse n'est point chiffrée: Les sixtes sont encore plus difficiles, a moins qu'une tres grande pratique avec un peu de goust ne supplée a la science. Je Suppose, que, pour entendre tous ce ci, l'on a quel*que* teinture de la musique vocale: Car, sans les premiers principes, Il y auroit bien des choses inintelligibles. Je suppose encor, que l'on scait, que toutes les parties hors la basse seule se joüent de la main droite. Le Plus sûr, c'est d'avoir un bon maistre, sans le quel il est bien difficile d'aprendre, si ce n'est a force de temps, et de patience: Les livres ne sont pas inutiles pour cela: Ils servent a Mettre l'Ecolier en estat d'interroger son maistre, et d'en tirer des Instructions, qui fortifient les Idées, que la speculation donne des premiers principes.

f. 5v

Du Mode, et de ses cordes essentielles.

Il y a quelques autheurs, qui traitent de la difference des accords, mais je n'en ay point vû, qui dise precisem*en*^{t} la raison, pour la quelle on dieze, ou on bemolize certaines nottes, dans la modulation la plus ordinaire du chant, et de la Musique Instrumentale; ce qui me paroist ce pendant si necessaire a sçavoir pour composer, et pour accompagner exactement, que l'on ne peut gagner l'un et l'autre sans cela, que par une longue estude, ou par une pratique encor plus longue. Les Regles suivantes le feront voir avec certitude la raison de la diversité de l'harmonie sur des Nottes de basses, qui semblent estre les mesmes les unes, que les aut*res*. Un autheur moderne definit le mode, une maniere de commencer, et conduire un chant par des cordes, qui sont affectées naturellement a une certaine corde et de le conclure, par cette mesme corde, que l'on appelle la finale.

One also calls mode "ton,"[6] but this is most improper, since the word *ton* ought to be intended only to express the distance from one sound to another, as in Ut to Re, Sol to La, etc. However, it is necessary to acknowledge that usage has decided it completely differently, and one says equally today that a piece is composed, for example, in the mode or *ton* of C sol ut or D la re, etc. although Ut or Re are only sounds that one knows by the

f. 6r

letters which precede them in the order of the scale, to help find them at a certain place on instruments. I will speak about it at more length elsewhere.

To know the mode in which a piece is composed, it is necessary to look at the last note of the bass. It is infallibly the note on which the modulation of all the others depends. The bass also almost always begins with the final, but the higher voices are not subject to this rule. [All the voices], however, normally come together on the final cadence.

There were several modes in music in the past. Today, they are reduced to two: namely, major mode and minor mode.

One calls major mode that of which the third is composed of two tones: C ut[7] is ordinarily the model. Minor mode is that of which the third is composed of a tone and of major semitone: D re[8] is ordinarily the model.

Therefore, what makes the major mode is the major third, and what makes the minor mode is the minor third. This note three scale degrees above the final is called the mediant.

The note five scale degrees above the final, which makes a perfect fifth, is called the dominant.

The note eight scale degrees above the final, which is the octave of the final, is equally called the final, because it is a repeat of the first sound.[9]

---

6. Key.

7. C major.

8. D minor.

9. An error is present in example c, as the mediant is labeled as the dominant and vice versa

On appelle aussy le Mode, Ton, mais c'est fort improprement, puis que le mot de Ton devroit estre seuleme*n*ᵗ destiné pour exprimer la distance, qui est d'un son a un autre, comme d'ut a Re, de Sol a La &c Cependant, il faut convenir, que l'usage en a decidé tout autrement, et que l'on dit egalement aujourdhuy, qu'une piece est composée, par exemple, dans le mode ou Ton de C sol ut, ou D la Re &c, quoyque Ut, ou Re ne soyent que des sons, que l'on connoist par les

f. 6r

lettres, qui les precedent dans l'ordre de la gamme, pour les Determiner sur les instrumens a un lieu certain: J'en parleray plus au long ailleurs:

Pour connoistre le mode dans le quel une piece est composée, il faut regarder la derniere notte de la basse, c'est infailliblement la corde, de la quelle la modulatio*n* de toutes les autres depend: La basse commence aussy presque toujours par la finale, Mais les dessus n'y sont point assujetis: Ils se trouvent pourtant ensemble a la finale pour l'ordinaire.

Il y avoit autrefois plusieurs Modes dans la musi*que*: aujourdhuy, ils sont reduits a deux: scavoir, mode majeur, et mode mineur.

On appelle mode majeur celuy, dont la Tierce est composée de deux Tons: C ut en est ordinairement le modelle: Mode mineur est celuy, dont la Tierce est composée d'un ton, et d'un semiton majeur: D re en est ordinairement le modelle:

Ce qui fait donc le mode majeur, c'est la Tierce Majeure: Et ce qui fait le mode mineur c'est la Tierce mineure: Cette notte elevée de trois degres au dessus de la finale, s'appelle mediante.

La note elevée de cinq degres au dessus de la finale, qui est la quinte juste, s'apelle dominante.

La note elevée de huit degres au dessus de la finale, qui est l'octave de la finale, s'apelle egalement finale, parce que c'est une replique du premier son. Ces

These three notes are marked thus in the majority of books that treat the first principles of music.

Mode majeur
[Major mode]

Mode min.
[Minor mode]

Fin.   Med.   Do.   Fi.
[Final] [Mediant] [Dominant] [Final]

F.   D.   M.   F.
[Final] [Dominant] [Mediant] [Final]

[Example b, f. 6v]

[Example c, f. 6v][9]

The sounds that go higher than the octave are only repeats of the first ones. Thus, the tenth is a third eight scale degrees higher, the eleventh a fourth eight scale degrees higher, and so on for the others.

Besides these principal notes of which we have just spoken, there are other essential notes in the mode that some call "favorite notes" and others call "sensitive notes."[10] The most "sensitive" is the semitone below the final. One could not land on the final without having played this note in the preceding chord.

In C sol ut it is B fa si-natural, [example] A. In D la re [it is] C sol ut-sharp, [example] B.

En C Sol ut
[In C major]

Do.   FIN.
[Dominant] [Final]

Do.   FIN.
[Dominant] [Final]

[Examples A and B, f. 6v]

This rule is infallible on any note of the scale on which the mode has been located. I think it pointless to give any more examples of this.

The tone above the final is as necessary as any other, but it would be difficult to change it, because the modulation protects it naturally.

In C sol ut it is Re, [example] C. In D la re [it is] Mi-natural, [example] D.

---

10. Hereinafter will be translated as "leading tone."

f. 6v

Ces [*sic*] trois cordes sont marquées ainsy dans la plus part des livres, qui traitent des premiers principes de musi*que*:

Mode majeur
[Major mode]

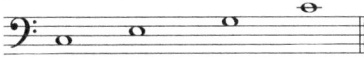

Mode min.
[Minor mode]

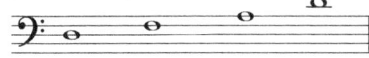

Fin.	Med.	Do.	Fi.
[Final]	[Mediant]	[Dominant]	[Final]

F.	D.	M.	F.
[Final]	[Dominant]	[Mediant]	[Final]

[Example b, f. 6v]

[Example c, f. 6v][9]

Les sons, qui vont plus haut, que l'octave ne sont que des repliques des premiers, ainsy la 10e. est une tierce huit degres plus haut, la 11. une quarte huit degres plus haut, et ainsy des autres:

Outre ces cordes principales, dont nous venons de parler, Il y a d'autres cordes Essentielles Au mode, que les uns nomment cordes favorites, les autres cordes sensibles: La plus sensible est le semiton au dessous de la finale; on ne sçauroit tomber a la finale, sans avoir touché cette corde dans l'accord precedent.

En c sol ut c'est b fa si ♮: A. En D la Re, c sol ut diezé. B.

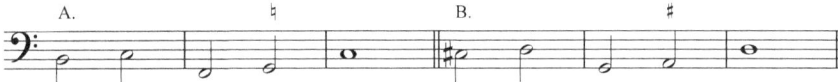

En C Sol ut	Do.	FIN.	Do.	FIN.
[In C major]	[Dominant]	[Final]	[Dominant]	[Final]

[Examples A and B, f. 6v]

Cette Regle est infaillible sur quelque corde de la gamme, que l'on ait placé son mode: Je croy inutile d'*en* multiplier Des exemples.

Le Ton d'au dessus la finale est aussy necessaire, qu'aucun autre, mais il seroit difficile de l'alterer, parceque la modulation le garde naturellement.

En C sol ut c'est Re C. En D la Re Mi ♮. D.

[Examples C and D, f. 6v]

It is the same in all the other keys.

The note four scale degrees above the final is called the fourth,[11] and [the interval] must be perfect. That is to say that in whatever mode it is, it must be composed only of two tones and a major semitone.

[Examples E and F, f. 6v][12]

In Ut [major] it is F, [example] E. In Re [minor] it is Sol, [example] F.[12]

f. 7r

It remains to speak of the note six scale degrees above the final, which is called the sixth,[13] and which is major or minor, depending on whether the third of the mode, called the mediant, is major or minor. It is composed of four tones and a major semitone in the major mode, and of three tones and two major semitones in the minor mode.

[Examples G and H, f. 7r]

---

11. I.e., subdominant.
12. The F in the third measure of this example should be an E.
13. I.e., submediant.

	C.			D.	
FI.	Ton d'audessus	FIN.	FIN.	Ton d'audess.	FIN.
[Final]	[Tone above]	[Final]	[Final]	[Tone above]	[Final]

[Examples C and D, f. 6v]

De mesme dans tous les autres Tons.

La notte distante de quatre degres au dessus de la finale s'apelle Quarte, et doit estre juste; c'est a dire, qu'en quelque mode que ce soit elle ne doit estre composée, que de deux tons et un semiton majeur

E	E.	F.	F.	F.	F.
	Quart.			Quart.	
	[Fourth]			[Fourth]	

[Examples E and F, f. 6v][12]

En ut c'est Fa E. En Re c'est Sol F.

f. 7r

Reste a parler de la Notte elevée de six degres au dessus de la finale, qu'on appelle sixte, et qui est majeure, ou mineure, selon que la Tierce du Mode, appelée mediante, est majeure, ou mineure: Elle est composée de 4. tons et un semiton majeur au mode majeur, et de trois tons et deux semitons Majeurs, au mode mineur

	G.				H.		
Fin	Sixte		FIN.	FIN.	Six.		FIN.
[Final]	du mode		[Final]	[Final]	[Sixth]		[Final]
	[Sixth of the mode]						

[Examples G and H, f. 7r]

In Ut [major] it is La, [example] G. In Re [minor] it is Si-flat, [example] H.

The note seven scale degrees above the final is a repeat of the leading tone of which I have already spoken, [example] A. I did not write a chapter about intervals because all the books on composition and accompaniment are in agreement on this point. It is explained very clearly in Nivers[14] and Masson,[15] among others.

It is important to remember what I have just said to understand harmonic order little by little.

In the following section it is necessary to explain the general principles to compose, or to realize chords on each of these notes in particular, choosing the harmony for them which is appropriate by the relationship which [the notes] have with the final of the mode in which one wants to work.

I do not speak of meter, since the first [exercise in] composing counterpoint is comprised of whole notes, which strictly speaking do not have [meter], and the slow movements of Corelli are played in this way at first by beginners. However, as a rule one uses **c** or **2** meter.

f. 7v

On the Method for Accompanying with the Harpsichord on a Bass, or for Writing One or More Parts on This Bass

I have already said that one is able to work with all the notes of the octave, and some authors have given examples of them. I think that it is necessary to indicate them more fully than has been done, so that one knows the way they are written according to the rules. I will speak only of those that are more commonly in use, reserving for a separate section to examine the different ways in which they can be written.

---

14. "This point" is addressed in the fourth and fifth chapters of Guillaume Gabriel Nivers's *Traité de la composition de musique* (Paris, 1667), 10–16. An explanation and examples of intervals are also found in Nivers's *L'Art d'accompagner sur la basse continue pour l'orgue et le clavecin* (Paris, 1689; repr., Geneva: Minkoff, 2000), 149–59, 154.

15. Intervals are described in Charles Masson's *Nouveau traité des règles pour la composition de la musique* (Paris, 1699; repr., New York: Da Capo Press, 1967), 3–6.

En ut c'est La G. En Re c'est Si♭. H.

La notte elevée de sept degres au dessus de la finale, est une replique du demyton favory, dont j'ay deja parlé. A. Je n'ay point fait un
chapitre des Intervalles, parce que tous les livres de composition, et
d'accompagnement sont tres d'accord sur cet article; Cela est expliqué fort clairement entr autres dans Nivers, et Masson.

Il est important de retenir ce que je viens de dire, pour concevoir
peu a peu l'ordre de l'harmonie.

Dans la division suivante, Il faut expliquer les principes generaux,
pour composer, ou pour accorder sur chacune de ces cordes en particulier, en choisissant l'harmonie, qui leur convient par le Rapport,
qu'elles ont avec la finale du Mode, dans le quel on veut travailler.

Je ne parle point de la mesure, puisque le premier contrepoint
de composition est de nottes rondes, qui n'en ont pas, aproprement
parler, Et que les airs graves de Corelli se joüent ainsy d'abord par les
commençans; Cependant on prend pour regle la mesure a C . ou a 2.

f. 7v

De la Methode pour accompagner au clavecin sur une basse, ou pour ecrire une ou plusieurs parties sur cette basse.

J'ay deja dit, qu'on pouvoit travailler sur Toutes les cordes de l'octave, et quelques autheurs en ont donné des Exemples. Je croy, qu'il
les faut marquer Plus au long, qu'ils n'ont fait, affin que l'on connoisse
la maniere de les Ecrire Regulierement: Je ne parleray, que de ceux,
qui sont plus en usage, me reservant a un article Separé d'examiner la
maniere differente, dont on peut ecrire les uns et les autres:

I believe I must explain why I do not give notes their ordinary names of C sol ut, of B fa si, of F ut fa, etc. The reason stems from the *Principles of Music* by Loulié.[16] He teaches us that since Ut and Re can be on all the notes of the scale by means of sharps and flats, it is pointless to call them C sol ut. Because sometimes, for the ease of the voices, music written in C sol ut is sung in Sol, since, according to the whim of the composer, this same music could be sung in Re, Fa, and La, and the note should therefore be called C re fa sol la ut.

This usage comes to us from plainchant. In plainchant, this usage is well founded, because there are only two ways to sing it: natural and soft.[17] In the natural [hexachord] C sol ut is called Ut, and in the soft [hexachord] Sol. But since in the past in plainchant, before having found the scale of Si, one was obliged to give a third name to C sol ut, and to name it C sol ut fa [*recte* C sol fa ut] in plainchant, because of mutation, knowledge of which

f. 8r

is useless today, and that finally this third name is out of use, and is found only in the [works of] old authors. Similarly, there is room to hope that people will gradually recognize the pointlessness of saying C sol ut, D la re, E si mi, F ut fa, G re sol, A mi la, B fa si, and [instead] will say C ut, D re, E mi, F fa, G sol, A la, B si, just as one commonly says Ut, Re, Mi, Fa, etc. But it is necessary to keep the letters which are at the beginning of these words, because they make known the [scale] degrees of the sounds, and without them one would have no rule for making oneself understood if one were to say, "I want to compose in Ut or in Re," because, since Ut and Re can be on any note, one can only assign the name of the note that one would ordinarily express by Ut or by Re by means of the letter that goes with it to mark the fixed place that it occupies on instruments.

---

16. Etienne Loulié's remarks on transposition are found in the second and third parts of his *Eléments ou principes de musique* (Paris, 1696; repr., Geneva: Minkoff, 1971), 29–31, 66–68.

17. The natural hexachord based on C is C D E F G A; the soft F G A B♭ E F. With the emergence of the scale of Si, the three traditional hexachords were supplanted by two heptachords: (1) the natural heptachord starting on C and (2) the soft heptachord on F.

Je croy devoir expliquer, pour quoy Je ne nomme pas les cordes du nom ordinaire de C sol ut, de B fa si, d'F ut fa &c La raison est tirée de Principes de Musique de Loulier. Il nous fait connoistre, que puisque ut et re peuvent estre sur toutes les cordes de la gamme par le moyen des diezes, et des b. mols, c'est inutilement, qu'on les apelle, C. Sol ut, parce que quelques fois, Pour la facilité des voix, de la musique ecrite en c. Sol ut se chante par Sol; puisque selon la fantaisie du compositeur, cette mesme musique pourra estre chantée par Re, par fa, ~~pa~~ par La; et la Notte devroit donc s'appeller C Re fa sol la ut.

Cet usage nous vient du plein chant: Et dans le plein chant cet usage est bien fondé, parce qu'il n'y a que deux manieres de le chanter, Sçavoir par nature, et par b.mol: en nature C. Sol ut s'appelle Ut, et par B.mol, Sol. Mais comme autrefois, dans le plein chant, avant d'avoir trouvé la gamme du Si, on estoit obligé de donner un troisieme nom a C Sol ut, et de le nommer C sol ut fa dans le plein chant, a cause des muances, dont la science

f. 8r

est inutile aujourdhuy, et qu'en fin ce troisieme nom est hors d'usage, et ne se trouve que dans les anciens autheurs, De mesme il y a lieu d'esperer, que peu a peu on reconnoistra l'inutilité de dire, C Sol ut, D la Re, E ssi [*sic*] mi, F. ut fa G re sol, A. mi la, B. fa si; Et l'on dira C. ut D. Re E mi F. fa. G. sol: A la B si, comme l'on dit communement ut re mi fa &c Mais il faut conserver les lettres, qui sont au commencement de ces mots, parce qu'elles font connoistre les degres des sons, et que sans elles ou n'auroit point de Regle pour se faire entendre, quand l'on diroit, je veux composer En. ut ou En re: Car puisqu'Ut et Re peuvent estre sur Toutes les cordes, on ne peut fixer le nom du son, que l'on esprime Ordinair*emen*^{t} par ut, ou par Re, que par la lettre, qui l'accompagne, pour marquer la place fixe, qu'il occupe sur les instrum*en*s.

It remains for us to say a word about the term transposition, which is no less ambiguous than "ton."

Most people call "transposed music" that which is not written in the keys which are close to diatonic order, among which C ut is the most natural, then F fa, G sol, D re, A la.

Thus, when they see C sol ut in minor, F fa and G sol also in minor, D re and A la in major, as in the following example,

| C. ut min. | F. fa mi. | G. sol mi. | D Re maj. | A la maj. |
| [C minor] | [F minor] | [G minor] | [D major] | [A major] |

[Example d, f. 8r]

without speaking of other more difficult keys, they call these keys

f. 8v

transposed music. Music transposed in this sense just means difficult music, because, when one plays music as written, however difficult it may be, that is to play it in its natural order. But when one plays it a semitone, a tone, or a third, etc. higher or lower, that is really to transpose it, because one is obliged to imagine another key than that which is written.

Here is the way to write each key with their essential notes.

1. C ut, which is naturally in major, is executed with two flats in minor. I think it would be pointless to explain the order of the flats and sharps. That is extremely well explained in the *Principles of Music* by L'Affilard, toward the end.[18]
2. D re, which is naturally in minor, is executed with two sharps in major.
3. E mi ♮: naturally in minor with one sharp; in major with four sharps. There is also E mi-flat: major with three flats.
4. F fa: naturally in major with one flat; in minor with three flats. There is also F fa-sharp minor with three sharps.

---

18. L'Affilard's *Principes* was first published in 1694 and reprinted many times until 1747. In the sections about transposition, the order of sharps and flats is explained and demonstrated. Michel L'Affilard, *Principes très faciles pour bien apprendre la musique* (Paris, 1705; repr., Geneva: Minkoff, 1979), 160–63.

Il nous reste a dire un mot sur le terme de Transposition, qui n'est pas moins Equivoque, que celuy du Ton.

La plus part des gens apellent de la musique transposée, celle qui n'est pas ecrite dans des Tons, qui aprochent de l'ordre diatonique, du nombre des quels C. ut est le plus naturel, puis F. fa, G. Sol, D Re. A La.

Ainsy, quand ils voyent C sol ut en Tierce mineure, F. fa et G sol aussy, En Tierce mineure, D re, et A la en Tierce majeure, comme dans l'exemple suivant

| C. ut min. | F. fa mi. | G. sol mi. | D Re maj. | A la maj. |
| [C minor] | [F minor] | [G minor] | [D major] | [A major] |

[Example d, f. 8r]

sans parler des autres Tons plus difficiles, ils appellent les tons de

f. 8v

la musique transposée. Musique transposée dans ce sens ne veut dire, que musique difficile; car, quand on joüe de la Musique comme elle est ecrite, quelque difficile qu'elle soit, c'est la joüer dans son ordre naturel; Mais quand on la joüe un semiton, un ton, une tierce &c plus haut; ou plus bas, c'est la veritablement transposer, parce qu'on est obligé de la figurer un autre Ton, que celuy qui est ecrit:

Voici la maniere d'ecrire chaque ton avec leurs cordes essentielles.

1. C ut, qui est naturellement en Tierce majeure, se traite en Tierce mineure avec deux b. mols: Je croy, qu'il seroit inutile d'expliquer l'ordre des b. mols et des diezes: cela est fort bien expliqué dans les principes de la musique par l'affilard, vers la fin.

2. D. Re, qui est naturellem*en*t en Tierce mineure, se traite en Tierce majeure avec deux diezes.

3. E. Mi, ♮. Nat*urellemen*t Tierce mineure avec un dieze, en Tierce Majeure avec 4. Die*z*es. Il y a encore E mi b. mol Tierce majeure avec 3. b. mols.

4. F. fa naturel en Tierce majeure avec un b. mol; en Tierce mineure avec trois b. mols: Il y a encor F. fa Diezé Tierce mineure avec 3. diezes.

5. G sol: naturally in major with one sharp; in minor with one flat.
6. A la: naturally in minor, is executed with three sharps in major.
7. B si ♮: [naturally] in minor with two sharps; in major with five sharps. This key is rare. B si-flat in major is more common, and must be written with two flats.

5. G. Sol nat*urel* en Tierce maj*eure* avec un Dieze, en Tierce mineure avec un b mol

6. A la nat*urel* en T. min*eure*, se traite en Tierce majeure avec
   trois diezes.

7. B. Si ♮. en T*ierce* min*eure* avec Deux diezes, en Tierce majeure
   avec cinq diezes: ce Ton est rare: B. Si b mol en Tierce ma-
   jeure est le plus commun, et doit s'ecrire avec deux b. mols.

f. 9r

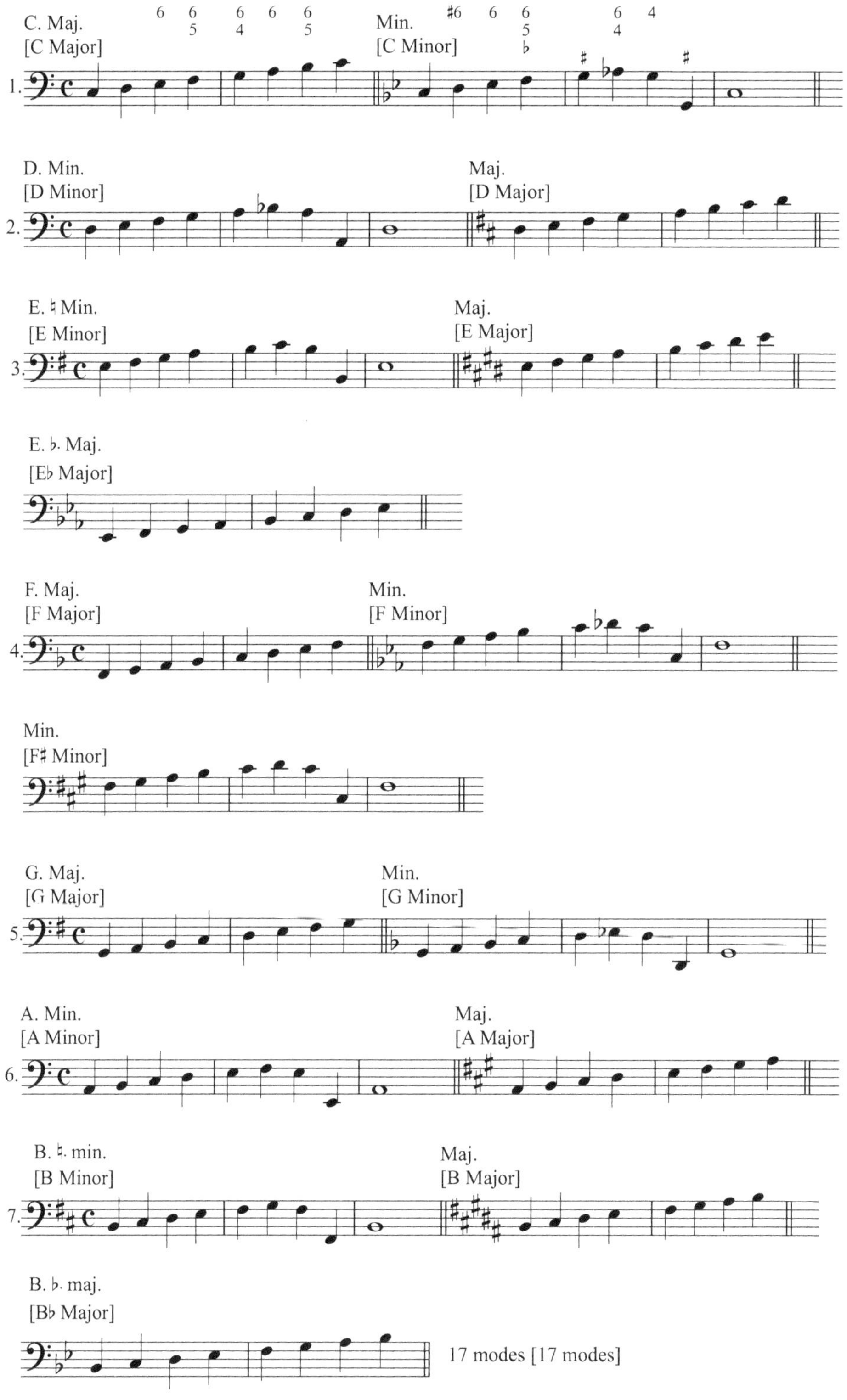

[Example e, f. 9r]

f. 9r

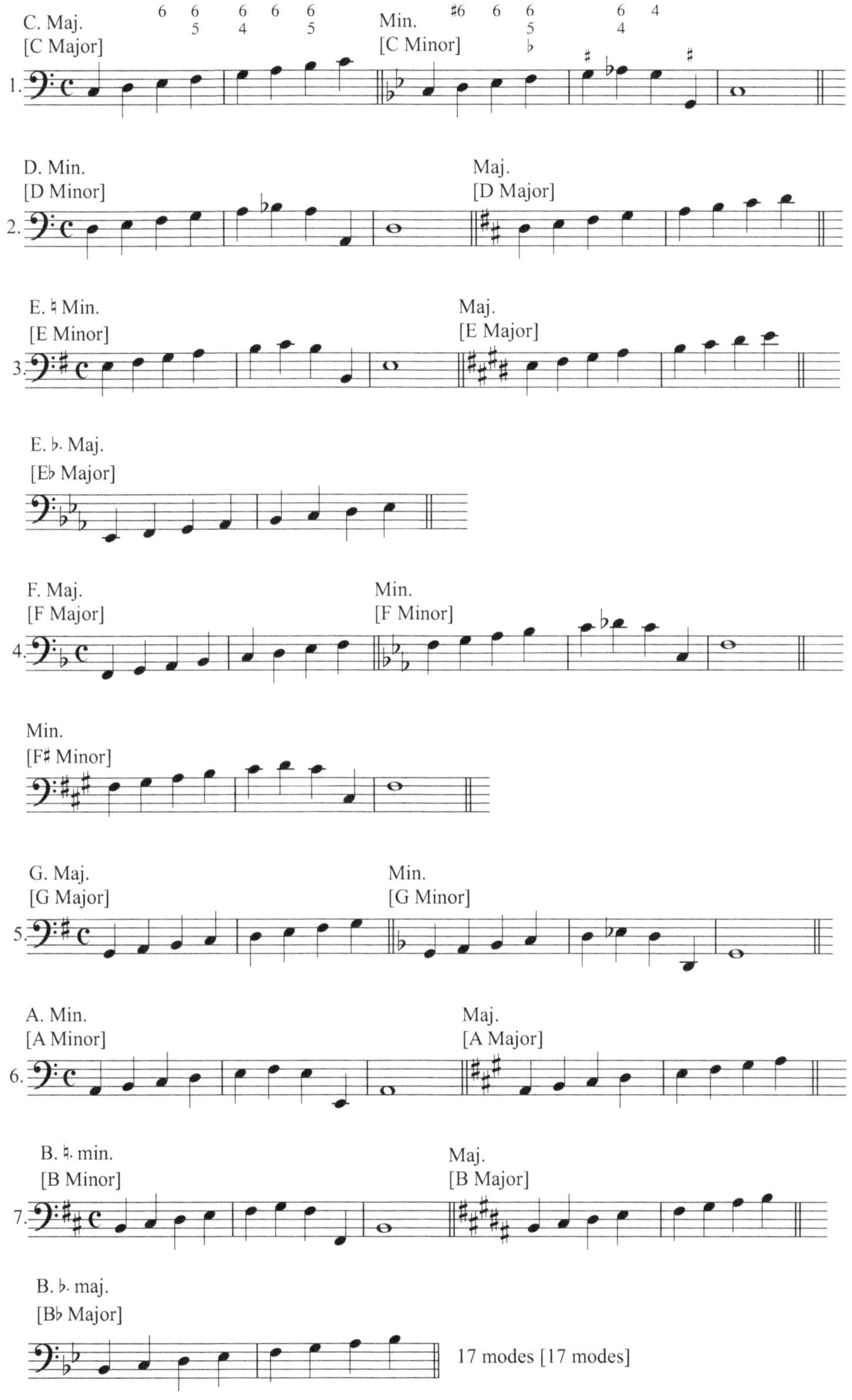

[Example e, f. 9r]

Perfect and Imperfect Chords

[blank staff paper]

One can write about the other notes, which are C ut-sharp [and] G re sol-sharp, but they are not in use because of their great difficulty, or rather, because they would be as inconvenient to play as to write.

After having gained a certain knowledge of the final or tonic (we have said that it is infallibly the last note of the bass of a cantata or of a sonata or the work in question).

On the leading tone, which this note has below it, and which one must always play in the chord that precedes the final.

On the whole tone which is above this final.

On the third, or mediant, which makes the mode major or minor when it is major or minor: that is to say, composed of two tones for the former, and of one tone and one semitone for the latter.

On the fourth, which must always be perfect: composed of two tones and one semitone.

On the fifth, or dominant, which is also always perfect: composed of three tones and one semitone.

And finally on the sixth, which is major or minor (composed of four tones and one semitone, or of three tones and two semitones), depending on whether the third is major or minor.

Of Consonances

It is necessary to know, then, which are the consonances that one can use for harmonizing [continuo parts], or for writing parts on these notes.

The perfect and imperfect consonances are:

f. 9v

des accords parf*aits* et Impar*fai*.^{ts}

[blank staff paper]

f. 10r

On peut ecrire sur les autres cordes, qui sont C ut diezé, G re sol diezé, mais cela n'est pas en usage a cause de la gr*an*de difficulté, ou plustost, parce qu'ils seroient aussy Incommodes a Joüer, qu'a Ecrire.

Apres avoir pris une connoissance certaine De la finale, ou corde du mode: (nous avons dit, que c'estoit infaillib*lemen*^t la derniere notte de la basse D'une cantate, ou d'une sonate, ou de l'ouvrage de Musique que ce soit.)

Du Demy ton favori, que cette corde a au dessous d'elle, et qu'*on* doit toujours toucher dans l'accord, qui precede la finale:

Du ton plein, qui est au dessus de cette finale

De la Tierce, ou Mediante, qui Rend la Mode Majeur, ou Mineur, quand elle est majeure, ou Mineure, *c'est* a*dire* composée de deux Tons pour l'un, et d'un Ton, et d'un demy ton pour l'autre.

De la quarte, qui doit toujours estre juste: co*m*posée de deux tons et un demy ton:

De la quinte, ou dominante, qui est aussy toujours Juste; composée de trois Tons et un semiton.

Et enfin De la Sixte, qui est majeure, ou mineure: (composée de quatre tons et un semiton, ou de trois tons et deux Demitons) selon, que la Tierce est maj. ou mineure.

Des consonances.

Il faut sçavoir ensuite, qu'elles sont les consonances, que l'on peut employer, pour accorder, ou pour ecrire des parties sur ces cordes:

Les consonances parfaites, et imparfaites, sont

the third, the fourth, the fifth, the sixth, [and] the octave. Musicians do not agree among themselves about which of these consonances are perfect or imperfect, with the exception of the fifth and of the octave, which all hold to be perfect consonances. But, regarding the third, the fourth, and the sixth, everyone gives different reasons for his opinion.

[Marginal note: Principles of Charpentier / First rule: No harmony without a third in several parts or against the bass.][19]

First, regarding the third, those who consider it to be a perfect consonance are touched by its beauty, beyond [the fact] that it is absolutely necessary [to include the third] in three parts and several parts, or against the bass, or between the parts.

[Marginal note: II. The sixth against the bass or between the parts takes the place of the third.][20]

But those who consider it to be an imperfect consonance, although they acknowledge its beauty and the necessity of using it for several parts, or against the bass, or between the parts, give a reason for it:

[Marginal note: There is a mean in all things, on either side of which, rectitude cannot exist. Horace, Sermones, I, 1, 106–7.]

The third allows augmentation and diminution, since it can be major and minor without ceasing to be a consonance. In contrast, the fourth, the fifth, and the octave allow neither augmentation nor diminution, without being altered; for the diminished and augmented fourth, the false and augmented fifth, and the diminished and augmented octave are dissonances.

---

19. Writer A appears to be familiar with Charpentier's writings, giving the impression that he knows the final six folios of the *Traité* were written by Charpentier. An abbreviation of this rule is found on f. 28r/f. 1r: "Point d'harmonie sans tierce." See also *Règles de composition par Mr Charpentier*: "Il n'y a point d'harmonie sans tierce; si ce n'est contre la basse, il faut que ce soit entre les parties." Catherine Cessac, *Marc-Antoine Charpentier* (Paris: Fayard, 2004), 472.

20. In a marginal note on f. 28r/f. 1r, Charpentier uses these words nearly verbatim ("la sixte entre les parties tient lieu de la tierce").

La Tierce: La Quarte, La Quinte, La Sixte l'octave. Les Musiciens ne sont pas d'accord entreux pour sçavoir les quelles de ces consonances sont parfaites, ou imparfaites, ~~au~~ a l'exception de la quinte, et de l'octave; que Tous tiennent, pour consonances parfaites: Mais, a l'egard de la Tierce de la quarte, et de la sixte, chacun donne de differentes raisons pour son opinion.

[Marginal note: Principes de Charpentier / I.ere Regle / Point d'harmonie sans tierce a plusieurs parties, ou contre la basse:]

Premierement, A l'egard de la Tierce, ceux, qui la Tiennent, pour une consonance parfaite, sont touchez par sa beauté, outre qu'elle est absolument necessaire a trois, & a plusieurs parties, ou contre la basse, ou entre les parties:

[Marginal note: II. La sixte contre la basse, ou entre les parties tient lieu de la Tierce:]

Mais ceux, qui la Tiennent pour consonance imparfaite, quoy qu'ils conviennent de sa beauté, et de la necessité de la pratiquer a plusieurs parties, ou contre la basse, ou entre les parties, En donnent une raison.

[Marginal note: Est modus in rebus, sunt certi denique fines, Quos ultrà citrà que nequit consistere rectum. hor. serm. lib. 1º. sat. 1.]

C'est que la Tierce souffre augmentation, et diminution, puisqu'elle peut estre majeure, et mineure sans cesser d'estre consonance; Au lieu, que la Quarte, la Quinte, et l'octave ne souffrent point ⁺augmentation ny diminution, sans estre alterées:⁺ car la quarte diminuée, et superflüe, la quinte fausse, et superflüe, l'octave diminuée, et superflüe sont des dissonances.[4]

---

4. The significance of the symbols surrounding the words "*augmentation ny diminution, sans estre alterées*" is unclear. There are interesting similarities between this phrase and one in Section B (f. 28r/f. 1r), where Charpentier writes "*acords parfaits 8 . 5 . et 4 et leurs repliques appellez parfaits parce quils ne souffrent ny augmentation ny diminution.*"

Regarding the sixth, as it is really an inverted third, one uses almost the same reasons for and against it.[21] However, it has one advantage, at least, over the third: that is, that one cannot begin [or] end a piece with the sixth, and that even in repose it must always be followed by the fifth or by the octave. It is this which will be explained at greater length below.

f. 11r

Regarding the fourth, opinions are even more varied [than those] regarding the third and the sixth. Some people make it mixed, that is to say, sometimes a consonance and sometimes a dissonance, according to the accompanying notes which one gives it. Other people want it to be a dissonance, because it must ordinarily be prepared and resolved as a dissonance. How to reconcile these two opinions with that which maintains that the fourth is a perfect consonance!

The foundation of this opinion is that the fourth is an inverted fifth, and that the fourth does not permit, any more than [the fifth], either augmentation or diminution without being altered; that it is not always necessary to prepare the fourth—as, for example, when it is with the sixth, many composers use it without preparation; that it is not always necessary to resolve it, as in the following example, as practiced by the Italians, [examples] A and B.[22]

[Examples A and B, f. 11r]

That finally, if one is nearly always obliged to follow it with some consonance, it has this necessity in common with the sixth, which so many people

---

21. Being considered perfect or imperfect; a consonance or a dissonance.

22. The figures in measure two appear to be in error. If the 6 of the 6/5/4 and the 8 of the 8/♭4/3 are interchanged, the voice leading is better. The ♭4 is also a mystery, as there appears to be no reason for it. This example is smudged and has been corrected in the manuscript, so perhaps it was not fully corrected.

A l'egard de la sixte, comme elle est proprement une Tierce renversée, on employe a peu pres les mesmes raisons pour et contre: Cependant elle a un avantage de moins, que la Tierce: c'est qu'on ne sçauroit commencer ny finir une piece par la sixte, et que mesme dans les
repos, elle doit toujours estre suivie de la quinte, ou de l'octave: C'est
ce qui sera expliqué plus au long dans la suite.

f. 11r

A l'egard de la quarte, les avis sont encor plus differens, qu'a l'egard
de la Tierce, et de la sixte. Les uns la font mixte, c'est a dire tantost
consonance, et tantost dissonance, selon les accompagnmens, qu'on
luy donne: Les autres veulent, qu'elle soit dissonance, parce qu'elle
doit estre ordinairement preparée, et sauvée comme une dissonance.
Comment accorder avec ces deux opinions celle, qui soustient, que
la Quarte est une consonan^{ce} parfaite!

Le fondement de cette opinion est, que la quarte est une quinte
renversée; et que la Quarte ne souffre non plus qu'elle, ny augmentation, ny diminution, sans estre alterée: Qu'il n'est pas toujours necessaire de preparer la quarte; comme par exemple, quand elle est avec la
sixte, bien des compositeurs l'employent sans preparation: Qu'il n'est
pas toujours necessaire de la sauver; comme dans l'exemple suivant,
ou elle est pratiquée par les Italiens A & B.

[Examples A and B, f. 11r]

Qu'enfin si l'on est presque toujours obligé de la faire suivre de
quelque consonance, cette necessité luy est commune avec la sixte,
que tant de gens

take for a perfect consonance.

That if one is obliged to prepare it as a dissonance when it is with the fifth, it would be necessary to say as well that the fifth is a dissonance when one joins it with the sixth, since one does not place the chord of a sixth and a fifth $\frac{6}{5}$ on a bass note, if the fifth is not prepared and resolved as a dissonance.

The consonance of a fourth is also played between the parts without being tied [i.e., suspended] or resolved.

This was the opinion of the late Charpentier. There are many skillful masters of contrary opinions, but it seems to me that practice can determine for us the treble in some manner.

All agree that these consonances produce perfect and imperfect chords. Let us see of what the perfect chord is composed.

The perfect chord is the third, fifth, and octave. Thus the third entering a perfect chord seems determined [as a] perfect consonance. But, considering the imperfect chord (which one forms with the third, sixth, and octave, or the fourth, sixth, and octave), with regard to the sixth, how can one view the sixth as a perfect consonance, since it gives the name to the imperfect chord?

Removing the fifth from the perfect chord changes the name of this chord. I am not, therefore, surprised if the chord 6 4 8 is called imperfect, since it derives its name from the sixth, and not from the fourth.

The fourth is therefore a perfect consonance for the reasons that we have just said. It serves in place of the fifth, and the ear often takes one for the other.

Finally, several of our instruments are tuned in fourths, as, for example, the treble and bass viol and the theorbo. It would seem ridiculous to me that one could think that an instrument might be tuned by dissonant intervals.

The perfect chord is made [in] only one way, i.e., 3 5 8. But there are two inversions besides that, i.e., 5 8 and 3; and 8 3 and 5. These three inversions produce the same harmony. One can see examples above, on page 16.[23]

---

23. Aside from the heading, "Perfect and Imperfect Chords," page 16 (f. 9v) is blank staff paper.

f. 11v

Tiennent pour une consonance parfaite.

Que si l'on est obligé de la preparer comme dissonance, quand elle est avec la Quinte, Il faudroit dire aussy, que la Quinte est dissonance, quand on la joint avec la sixte, puisque l'on ne place point l'accord de sixte, et quinte $^{6}_{5}$ sur une notte de basse, que la quinte ne soit preparée, et sauvée comme une dissonance.

La Quarte consonance se pratique encor entre les parties, sans estre liée, ny sauvée.

C'estoit la l'opinion de feu[5] Charpentier. Il y a de fort habiles maistres des opinions contraires: Mais, Il me semble, que l'usage peut nous determiner en quelque façon la dessus.

Tous conviennent, que ces consonances produisent l'accord parfait, & Imparfait. Voyons de quoy, l'accord parfait est composé.

Laccord parfait est Tierce, Quinte, et Octave. Ainsy la Tierce entrant dans l'accord parfait semble determinée consonance parfaite: Mais, considerant l'accord Imparfait, (que l'on compose de Tierce, sixte, et octave, ou de quarte, sixte, et octave) A l'egard de la sixte; comment peut on la regarder, comme consonan^{ce} parfaite, puis qu'elle donne le nom a laccord Imparfait?

f. 12r

En retranchant la quinte de l'accord parfait, Elle le fait changer ces accord de nom: Je ne suis donc pas surpris, si l'accord 6. 4. 8. est appellé imparfait, puisqu'il tire son nom de la sixte, et non de la Quarte.

La Quarte est donc consonance parfaite par les raisons, que nous venons de dire: Elle tient lieu de la Quinte, et l'oreille les prend souvent l'une pour l'autre:

Enfin plusieurs de nos Instrumens sont accordez a la quarte, comme *Par Ex*ample le dessus, et la basse de viole, & le theorbe: Il me paroistroit ridicule, qu'on pûst penser, qu'un Instrument fust accordé par Intervalles de Dissonances.

L'accord parfait ne se fait, que d'une maniere, sçavoir 3. 5. et 8. Mais Il a Deux faces; outre celleci: sçavoir. 5. 8. et 3. 8. 3. et 5. Ces trois faces produisent la mesme harmonie.

on peut voir les examples cy dessus page 16:

---

5. In the manuscript it looks as if the author began to write "Ch," then wrote "*feu*" over it. Charpentier, who died on 24 February 1704, is the only composer or theorist referred to as "*feu*," when others mentioned were also deceased (e.g., Lully, Masson).

The imperfect chord is made in three ways, and each way has its various inversions: i.e.,

3 6 8 | 6 8 and 3 | 8ve 3 6 |

Second way: 4 8 6 | 8 6 4 | 6 4 8 |

Third way: when one doubles the sixth with the third, or the third with the sixth by removing the octave: 6 3 6 | 3 6 3 |

Let us see which of these chords one chooses for each note

f. 12v

of the mode.

Chords on the Notes of the Mode

1. The final requires [a] perfect chord, [example] A.[24]
2. The whole tone above the final requires an imperfect chord made up of 6 8 and 3, [example] B, or else two sixths and a third, or two thirds and a sixth. Ibid.
3. The major or minor third: imperfect chord: 6 8 3, [example] C.
4. The perfect fourth: perfect chord, [example] D. With minor mode, the fourth carries a minor third.
5. The perfect fifth: perfect chord (It imitates the final.), [example] E.
6. The sixth, major or minor according to the nature of the third, also requires the same chord as it [the third] does, [example] F.
7. The major seventh of the key, which is the leading tone, requires an imperfect chord such as that of the sixth: i.e., either 6 8 3 or two sixths doubled with the third, or two thirds doubled with the sixth, [example] G.

Exceptions

After having established these first principles, it is necessary to pay attention to the following exceptions:

The bass progresses or proceeds by conjunct degrees (that is to say, by step, e.g., ut, re, mi, fa, sol, etc.), or else it proceeds by disjunct degrees, i.e., by leap.

The easiest basses are those which proceed by leap. Then one plays a perfect chord on all the notes, [example] H.

---

24. Example A is found on f. 13r/p. 23.

L'accord Imparfait se fait de trois manieres, et chaque maniere a ses faces differentes: sçavoir 3. 6. 8. | 6. 8. et 3. | 8.^{ve} 3. 6. |

Seconde maniere 4. 8. 6: | 8. 6. 4. | 6. 4. 8: |.

Trois*ieme* maniere; quand on double la sixte avec la Tierce, ou la Tierce avec la sixte en retranch l'8.^{ve} 6. 3. 6. | 3. 6. 3. |

Voyons les quels de ces accords on choisit pour chaque corde

f. 12v

du mode:

Accords sur les cordes du Mode:

1. La finale veut Accord parfait   A
2. Le Ton entier au dessus de la finale veut l'accord imparfait composé de 6. 8. et 3. B   ou bien deux sixtes, et une Tierce, ou deux Tierces, et une sixte. Ibid.
3. La Tierce majeure ou mineure, Accord imparf. 6. 8. 3.   C
4. La Quarte Juste, Accord parfait. D   au mode mineur la quarte porte Tierce mineure.
5. La Quinte juste; Accord parfait (Elle imite la finale:) E
6. La Sixte, Majeure ou Mineure selon la nature de la Tierce, demande Aussy le mesme accord qu'elle. F.
7. La septieme majeure du Ton, qui en est le semiton sensible demande l'accord imparfait tel, que celuy, de la sixte: *C'est adire* ou 6. 8. 3. ou 2. sixtes doublées avec la Tierce, ou deux Tierces doublées avec la sixte G.

Exceptions

Apres avoir posé ces premiers principes, Il faut faire attention aux Exceptions suivantes:

La Basse module, ou procede par degrez conjoints, c'est a dire de suite, comme ut, re, mi, fa, sol, &c ou bien elle procede par degrez disjoints, *C'est adire* Eloignez.

Les basses les plus aisées sont celles, qui procedent par Degrez disjoints, alors sur toutes les nottes, on joüe accord parfait. H.

f. 13r/p. 23

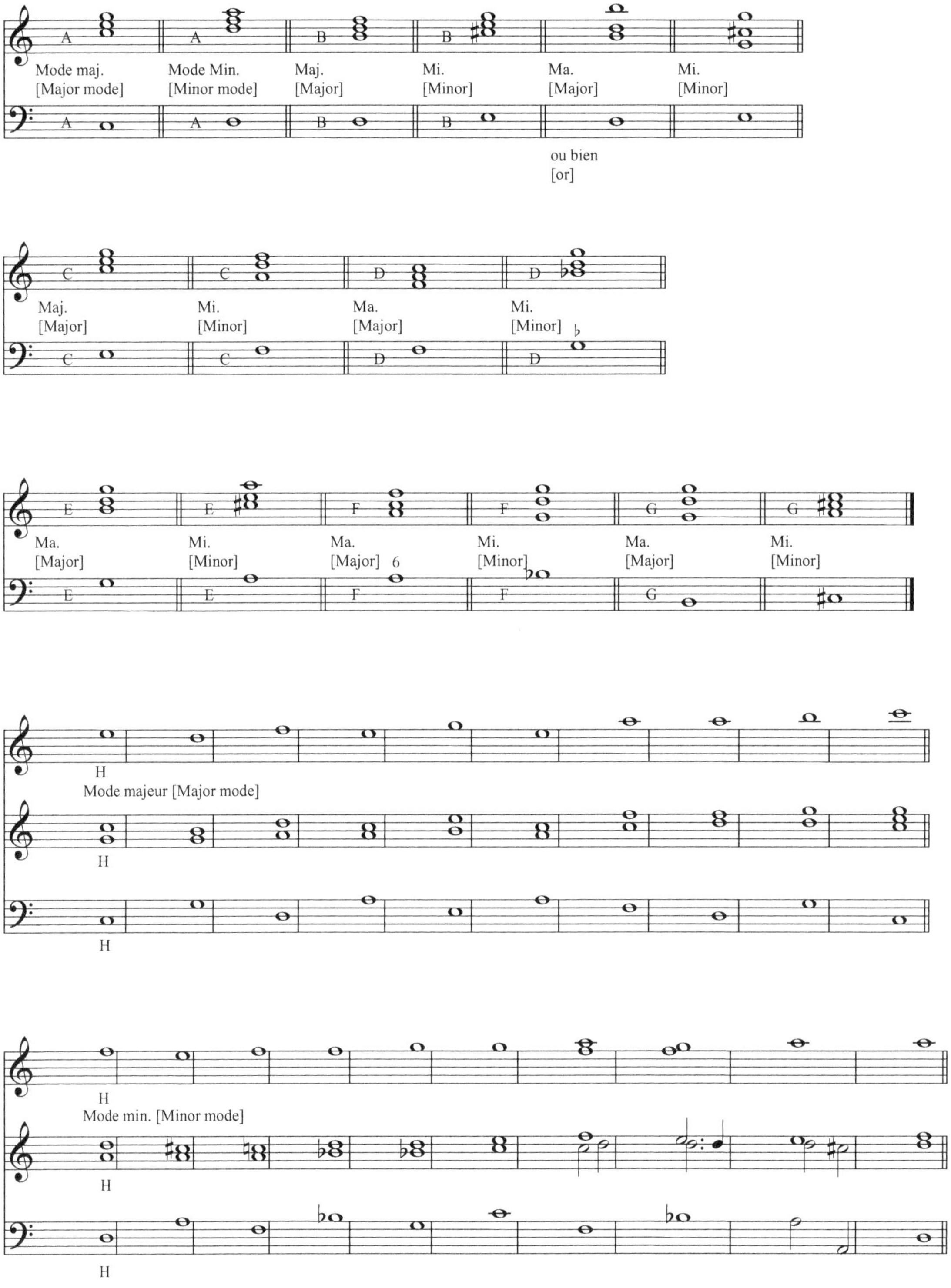

[Examples A through H, f. 13r/p. 23]

f. 13r/p.23

Mode maj. [Major mode] — Mode Min. [Minor mode] — Maj. [Major] — Mi. [Minor] — Ma. [Major] — Mi. [Minor]

ou bien [or]

Maj. [Major] — Mi. [Minor] — Ma. [Major] — Mi. [Minor]

Ma. [Major] — Mi. [Minor] — Ma. [Major] — Mi. [Minor] — Ma. [Major] — Mi. [Minor]

Mode majeur [Major mode]

Mode min. [Minor mode]

[Examples A through H, f. 13r/p. 23]

f. 13v/p. 24

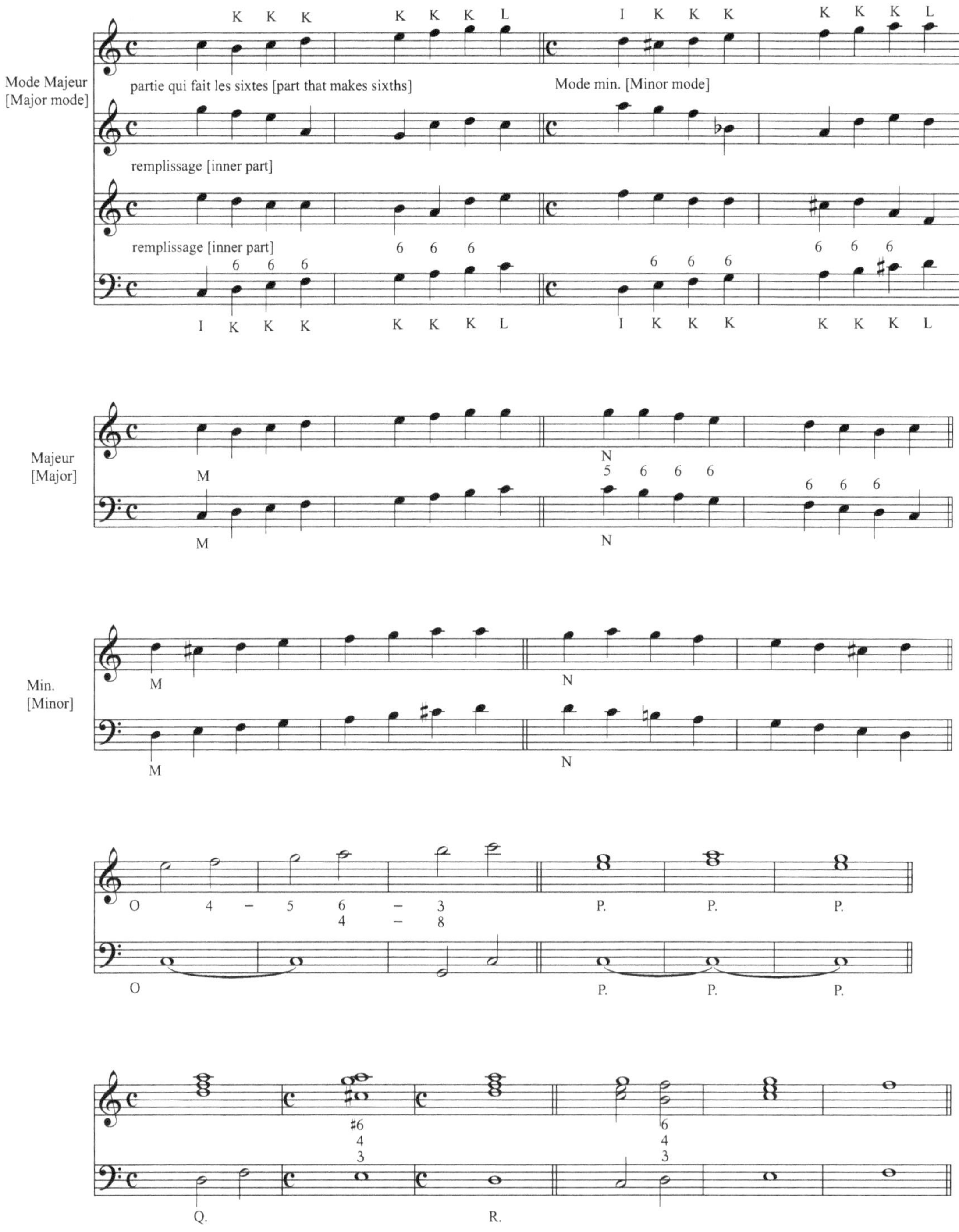

[Examples I through R, f. 13v/p. 24]

f. 13v/p. 24

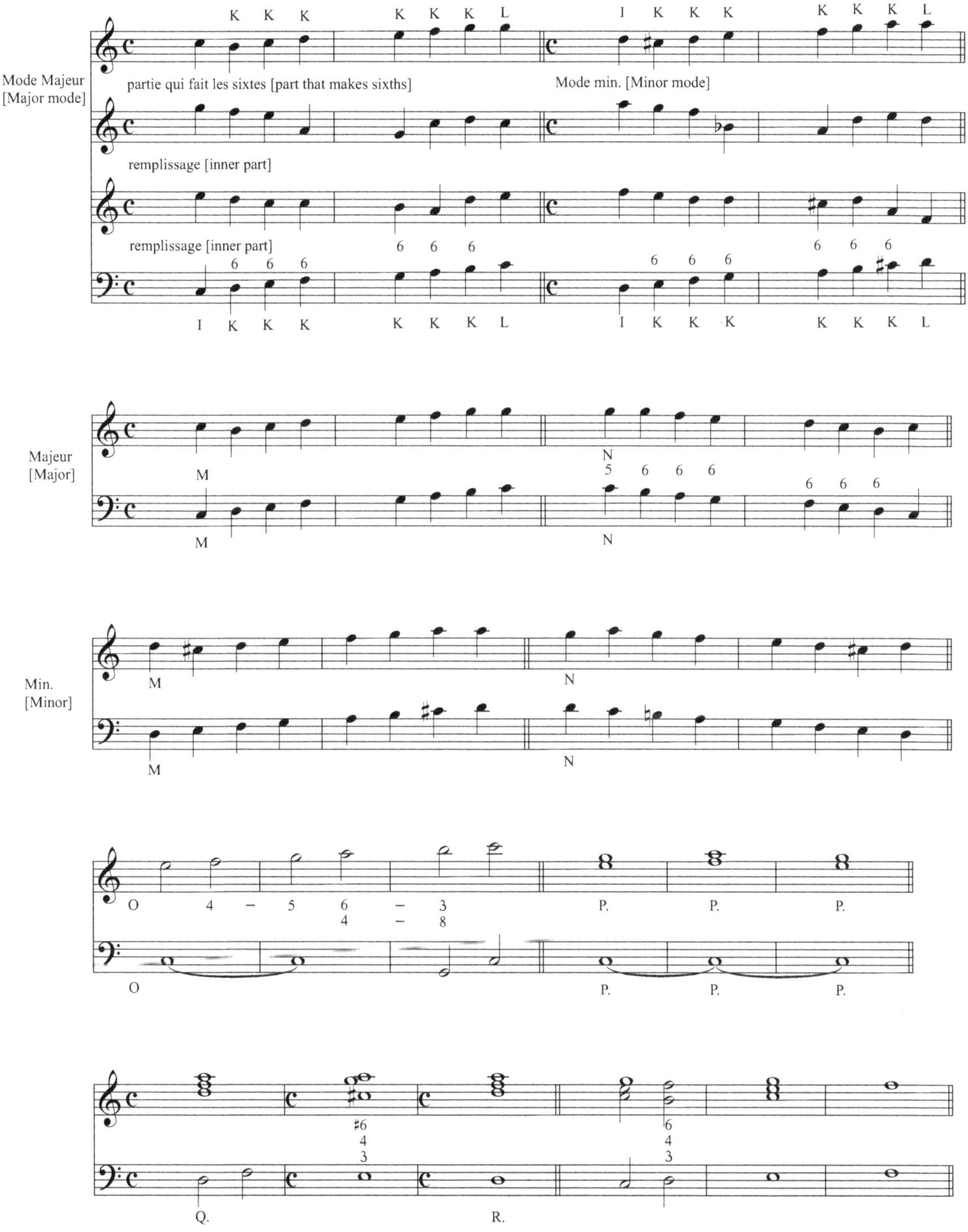

[Examples I through R, f. 13v/p. 24]

f. 14r/p. 25

When the bass proceeds by step, ascending or descending, if it rises continuously, one ordinarily plays them all as sixths, [example] K, after the perfect chord on the first note, [example] I, until the bass stops, [example] L, in which case one plays a perfect chord.

One sees by these examples that an imperfect chord must always be followed by a perfect, because one cannot stop on the imperfect chord.

The perfect chord is in music [equivalent to] the period in speech.

There are two ways to play the imperfect chord. The first is that which we have seen until now, when the bass rises, [example] M, or descends by step in major or minor mode, [example] N.

The second [is] when the bass stays [on the same pitch], and the treble moves, [example] O, or descends again to the perfect chord immediately afterwards, [example] P.

That is one of the ways of playing the consonant fourth without preparation in the treble, [presumably example O].

There is another new way of playing the fourth with the third without resolving it in the treble or in the bass, [examples] Q and R.

This way is convenient for avoiding errors in accompaniment, but is rare in written music.

f. 14v/p. 26

Observation

I have already said that a person who accompanies can begin the chords of the right hand with that of three [positions: root and inversions] that he wants to choose for his convenience:

The composer, in the course of the melody of a piece, also has the freedom to choose the one which pleases him the most for the flow of the melody. But it is necessary, as much as one can, to favor the third over the fifth, and the fifth over the octave. The octave itself is not a very sensitive interval. The unison is even less [so]. One only uses these intervals to connect the melody or to prepare dissonances. But it is absolutely necessary to avoid the unison of a melody with the bass.[25]

---

25. I.e., do not double the melody.

f. 14r/p. 25

Quand la basse procede par degrez conjoints, en montant, ou en descendant: Si elle monte sans aucun repos, on y fait ordinairement toutes sixtes, K. apres l'accord parfait sur la premiere note I., jusqu'a ce que la basse se repose. L. auquel cas on y fait l'accord parfait.

Lonvoit[6] par ces exemples, que l'accord Imparfait doit toujours estre suivi du parfait, parce qu'on ne peut se reposer sur l'accord Imparfait.

L'accord parfait est dans la musique, le point dans le discours.

Il y a deux manieres de pratiquer l'accord Imparfait: La premiere est celle, que nous avons vüe jusques a present, quand la basse monte, M., ou descend par degrez conjoints. En mode Majeur, ou Mineur. N.

La seconde, quand la basse demeure, Et que le dessus chemine, O: ou retombe a l'accord parfait aussytost apres P.

Voila une des manieres de pratiquer la quarte consonante sans preparation au dessus:

Il y a encor une maniere nouvelle de pratiquer la quarte avec la Tierce, sans la sauver au dessus, ny a la basse. Q. R.

Cette maniere est commode pour Eviter les fautes, dans l'accompagnement, mais elle est rare dans la musique. Ecrite:

f. 14v/p. 26

Observation.

J'ay deja marqué, qu'une personne, qui accompagne, peut commencer les accords de sa main droite par celuy des trois, qu'elle veut choisir pour sa commodité:

Le compositeur, dans la suite du chant d'une piece a aussy la liberté de choisir celuy, qui luy plaist le plus, pour la liaison du chant; Mais Il faut tant qu'on peut, preferer la Tierce a la Quinte, et la quinte a l'octave: L'octave est mesme un accord peu sensible: Lunisson est encor moindre; on ne s'en sert de l'un et de lautre de ces accords, que pour lier le chant, ou pour la preparation des dissonances: Mais Il faut eviter absolument l'unisson d'un chant de dessus avec la basse:

---

6.   I.e., L'on voit.

One ordinarily gives a routine rule to beginners: that is, to play first only thirds over the bass that they are given to work on, then to combine them with sixths, and later other consonances, except the fourth, for which a particular instruction is needed.

These observations are accepted in all the composition treatises, and I got [that information] from the late Charpentier and from Loulié.

f. 15r/p. 27

On the Way to Cadence on Every Note of the Mode, and Which Are the Notes That It Is Necessary to Choose.

After the cadence on the final, the most natural in all the modes is the cadence on the dominant.

This cadence is played like that which is made on the final, so that it is no longer necessary to think in some way about the final, and to consider as its final that [note] where one wants to make a cadence.[26]

En c sol ut
[In C major]

Dominante
ou l'on va cadencer.
[Dominant cadence]

[Examples A through G, f. 15r/p. 27]

We have explained above that note A is the leading tone of the mode, note B the fourth of the mode, and C the dominant.

Likewise, the dominant, C, has its leading tone, D, and its fourth, E, and its dominant, F, and its final, G, and so on for the other notes.

Each note on which one is going to cadence in the major or minor mode, therefore, has the same fundamental notes[27] as the final does: that is to say, a semitone below it, the whole tone above, its third, its sixth, its fourth, and its fifth.

---

26. I.e., treat the cadence on the dominant in the same way as that on the final.
27. I.e., scale degrees.

On donne ordinairement une regle de routine aux commençans: c'est de faire d'abord des Tierces seulement sur la basse, qu'on leur donne pour travailler, puis d'y mesler les sixtes, et par la suite les autres consonances, a la reserve de la quarte, pour laquelle Il faut une instruction particuliere:

Ces observations sont reçües dans touts les Traitez de composition, et je les Tiens de feu charpentier et de Loulier.

f. 15r/p. 27

De la Maniere de Cadencer
a chaque corde du Mode, et quelles sont les
cordes, qu'il faut choisir.

Apres La cadence a la finale, la plus naturelle dans tous les modes est la cadence a la dominante.

Cette Cadence se pratique comme celle, que se fait a la finale, Ensorte, qu'il ne faut plus songer en quelque façon a la finale, et considerer comme sa finale, celle, ou l'on veut faire cadence.

En c sol ut
[In C major]

Dominante
ou l'on va cadencer.
[Dominant cadence]

[Examples A through G, f. 15r/p. 27]

Nous avons expliqué cy devant, que la Notte A est le semyton sensible, ou favori du mode, La Notte B. La quarte du mode, et C. la dominante:

Demesme, la dominante C. a son semiton favori D. et sa quarte E. et sa dominante F. et sa finale G. et ainsy des autres cordes:

Chaque notte, ou l'on va cadencer En mode maj. ou mineur a donc chacune en particulier ses cordes essentielles comme la finale: c'est adire un demiton au dessous d'elle, le Ton plein au dessus, sa Tierce, sa sixte, sa quarte, et sa quinte.

f. 15v/p. 28

However, although each cadence is like the period in discourse, it always has some relationship with the final of the piece. This is why every note must be treated as major or minor, according to the place that it occupies among the fundamental notes of the mode that one is dealing with. Example H, I.

In the major mode, the dominant also can be treated equally as major or minor, [example] H, I.

The cadence on the tone above the final, which is Re in C ut, must be treated as minor, [example] K.

The cadence on the sixth of the major mode is also treated as minor, [example] L.

The cadence on the mediant of the major mode is also treated as minor, [example] M.

The cadence on the fourth and on the whole tone below the tonic should not be practiced at first.

In the Minor Mode

The dominant is always treated as minor, like the final, [example] N.

The cadence on the mediant is always major, [example] O.

The cadence on the tone below the mode is also major,
    [example] P.

The cadence on the fourth is minor, like the tonic, [example] Q.

The cadence on the sixth of the mode is treated (like that of the
    third, or mediant) as major, [example] R.

It is necessary to return to the final to finish.

Cependant, quoyque chaque cadence soit comme la periode dans le discours, elle a toujours quelq*ue* rapport a la finale de la piece: c'est pourquoy chaque corde doit estre traitée en Tierce majeure, ou mineure, selon la place, qu'elle occupe parmi les cordes essentielles du mode que l'on Traite: Exemple. H. I.

Au mode majeure, la dominante peut estre egalement traitée en Tierce majeure ou mineure: H. I.

La cadence au Ton d'au dessus la finale, qui est re, en C. ut doit estre traité en Tierce min. K.

La Cadence a la Sixte du mode majeur est aussi traitée en tierce mineure L.

La cadence a la Mediante du Mode majeur, est aussy traitée en tierce mineure M.

La Cadence a la Quarte, et au Ton plein au dessous de la corde du mode ne doivent pas estre pratiq*uée* d'abord.

Au Mode mineur.

La dominante est Toujours traitée en T*ierce* min*eure* comm*e* la final*e*. Ex*ample* N.

La cadence a la Mediante est touj*ours.* maj*eure*. Ex*ample* O.

La cadence au Ton au dessous du Mode est Aussy maj*eure*. P.

La Cadence a la quarte est min*eure* comm*e* la corde du mode. Q.

La cadence a la sixte du mode est traitée (comme celle de la Tierce, ou Mediante) en Tierce maj*eure* R.

Il faut retourner Ensuite a la finale p*our* finir

f. 16r/p. 29

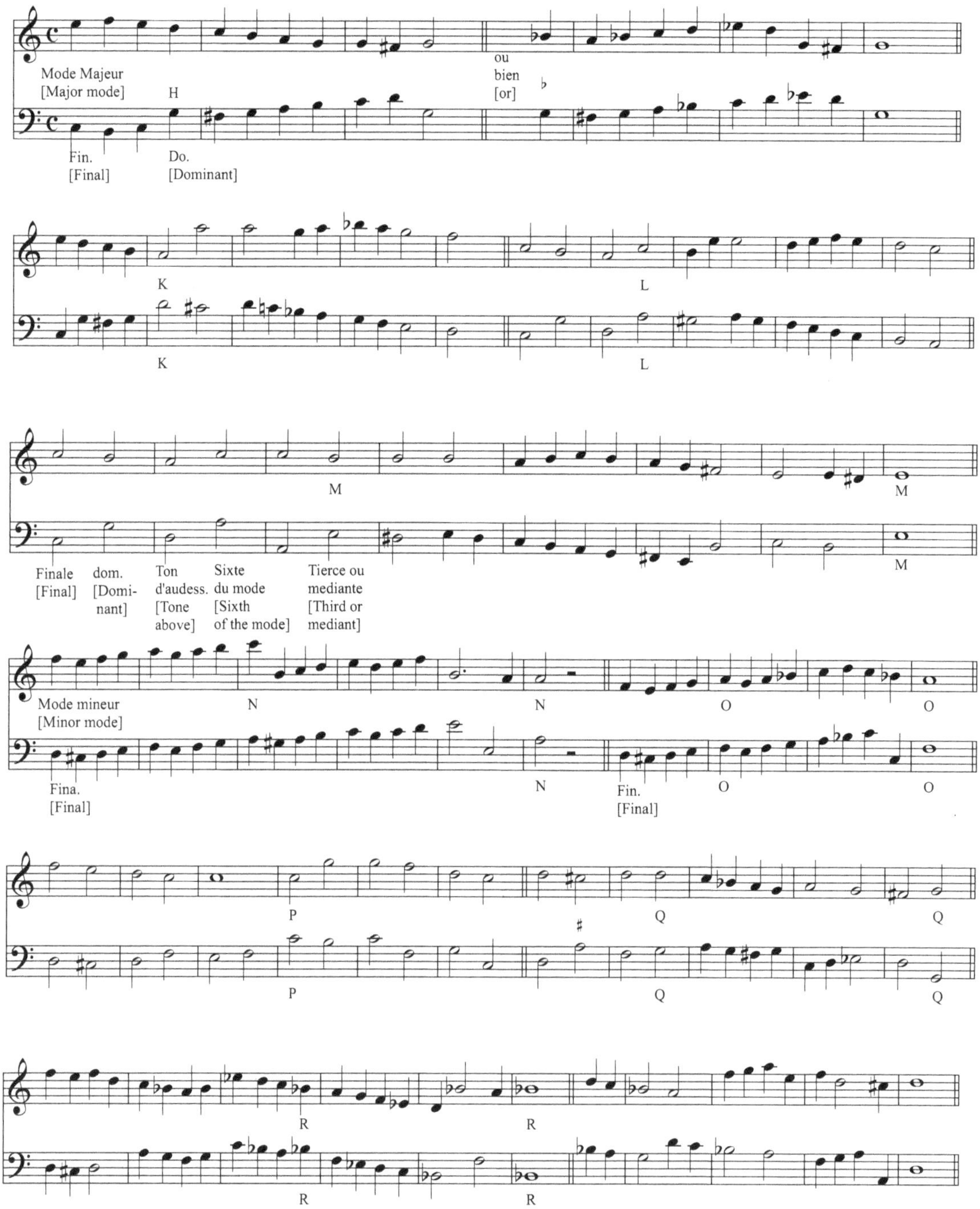

[Examples H through R, f. 16r/p. 29]

f. 16r/p. 29

Mode Majeur
[Major mode]   H

ou bien
[or]

Fin.   Do.
[Final]   [Dominant]

K   L

K   L

M

Finale   dom.   Ton   Sixte   Tierce ou
[Final]   [Domi-   d'audess. du mode   mediante
          nant]   [Tone   [Sixth   [Third or
                    above]   of the mode] mediant]

Mode mineur   N   N   O   O
[Minor mode]

Fina.   N   Fin.   O   O
[Final]   [Final]

P   Q   Q

P   Q   Q

R   R

R   R

[Examples H through R, f. 16r/p. 29]

f. 16v/p. 30

[blank staff paper]

f. 17r/p. 31

On the Choice That It Is Necessary to Make between the Major and Minor Mode

It is quite inconsequential whether one chooses, either for composing or for accompanying, the major mode or the minor. However, I believe that the major mode is preferable. It is simpler and more regular in its modulation. Its expression is cheerful.

The expression of the minor mode is more tender and sadder. It is irregular in its modulation, and this irregularity produces more cadences than in the major mode, and gives occasion to vary [them] to advantage.

On the Order of the Cadences

After having demonstrated all the possible cadences, [it] remains to show from them the most natural order: a useful thing for forming the imagination of beginners; because those who are more advanced in composition often neglect these rules.

These are, however, founded on experience and on use, and I got them from a master of today whose works have universal approbation.

I mark the dominant thus: Do. The tone above the final thus: Dv. The tone below: Dov. The sixth: S. The mediant: M. The final: Fi.

f. 16v/p. 30

[blank staff paper]

f. 17r/p. 31

Du choix, qu'il faut faire du mode
majeur, ou du mode mineur

Il est assez indifferent de choisir d'abord, p*our* composer, ou pour accompagner, le mode majeur, ou mineur. Cependant, je croy, que le mode majeur est preferab*le*. Il est plus simple, et plus regulier dans sa modulation. Son expression est gaye:

L'expression du mode mineur est plus tendre et plus triste: Il est irrigulier dans sa modulation, et cette irregularité produit plus ca-dences, qu'au mode majeur, et donne occasion de diversifier d'ava*n*-tage.

De l'ordre des cadences

Apres avoir demontré toutes les cadences possibles, reste d'en de-monstrer l'ordre le plus natural: chose utile pour fixer l'imagination des commençans: car, a l'egard de ceux, qui sont avancez dans la com-position, Ils negligent souvent ces Regles:

Elles sont pourtant fondées sur l'experience, et sur l'usage; Et je les tiens d'un maistre de ce temps, dont les ouvrages ont une appro-bation universelle:

Je marque la dominante ainsy Do: le Ton d'au dessus la finale ainsy: Dv. le Ton d'au dessous Dov. la sixte S. la Mediante M. la fi-nale Fi.

f. 17v/p. 32

The order of the major mode is to cadence on the dominant, which is Sol in C ut

Then on the tone above, which is Re

On the sixth of the mode, which is La

On the mediant, or third of the mode, which is Mi.

See this demonstration of these cadences above, [example] S.[28]

When one wants to cadence on the fourth of the major mode, one can go there after the dominant (I) or after the final itself (II).

To cadence on the whole tone below the mode, there is not a single example in the first four opuses of Corelli. Thus, I give no examples.

One can, however, go there from the fourth of the mode. The sounds on which one does not make a cadence are Ut-sharp, Mi-flat, Fa-sharp, Sol-sharp, and Si-natural, or the notes that represent them in the different modulations of the major mode.

Observation

Note that the way [to make] cadences in the major mode leads the melody from fifth to fifth: from Ut to Sol, from Sol to Re, from Re to La, which is, strictly speaking, to go from dominant to dominant. But, the way [to make] cadences in the minor mode is not entirely the same.

f. 18r/p. 33

The order of the minor mode is to go from the final to the mediant, Fa

From the mediant, to the tone below the mode, which is Ut

From the tone above to the dominant, which is La

From the dominant, to the fourth, which is Sol

From the fourth to the sixth, which is Si-flat, then cross it again
   to the mediant, to finish with the final.

See example T.[29]

---

28. Example S is missing.
29. Example T is missing.

f. 17v/p. 32

L'ordre de Mode Majeur est de cadencer a la dominante qui est Sol en C ut

Puis au Ton D'au dessus, qui est Re

A la sixte Du mode, qui est La

A la Mediante, ou Tierce du mode, qui est Mi.

Voyez cy devant la demonstration de ces cadences: S

Quand on veut cadencer a la quarte du mode maj*eur*, on y peut aller apres la dominante. I. ou apres la finale mesme II.

Pour cadencer au Ton plein au dessous du mode, il n'y en a pas un seul exemple dans les 4. premiers œuvres de Corelli: Ainsy, Je nen donne point d'exemples:

On y peut pourtant aller de la Quarte du Mode. Les sons, aux quels on ne fait point de cadence sont ut diezé, Mi b. mol fa diezé, sol diezé et Si ♮., ou bien les sons, qui les representent dans les differentes modula*t*ions du mode Majeur.

Observation.

Remarquez, que la Methode des cadences au Mode majeur conduit le chant de Quinte en Quinte: D'ut a Sol. de Sol a Re: du Re au La: Ce qui est, proprement parlant, aller de dominante en dominante, mais la methode des cadences au Mode mineur n'est pas tout a fait la mesme.

f. 18r/p. 33

L'ordre du mode mineur Est d'aller de la finale a la mediante Fa

De la Mediante, au Ton d'au dessous le mode, qui est Ut.

Du Ton d'au dessus a la Dominante, qui est La

De la dominante a la quarte, qui est Sol

De la Quarte, a la sixte, qui est si b. mol. puis repasser a la Medi-
    ante pr. finir par la finale.

Voyez l'Exemple T.

Observation

Note that in the major mode[30] one does not go directly to the mediant [E], because the semitone which the mediant requires [i.e., D-sharp], alters the upper leading tone, which is Re-natural [D-natural]; because it is necessary to sharpen it [in order] to cadence on the mediant. But, in the minor mode,[31] one goes directly to the mediant without preparation, because Mi, which is the tone above the final, is naturally the semitone of the mediant, Fa.

Also, one does not go from fifth to fifth in the minor mode,[32] because after having gone from the final to the dominant, and from the dominant to the tone above the mode, which is Mi, to go to the perfect fifth, which is Si-natural, it would be necessary to play Si in its natural position, which the modulation of the minor key prohibits.[33]

f. 18v/p. 34

It is necessary, therefore, to take it as a rule that, as in the major mode the modulation leads the cadences from fifth to fifth, in the minor mode the modulation leads the cadences from third to third, although that is not obligatory.

On the Notes That Seem Ambiguous

One is sometimes surprised to see that basses whose notes seem the same require different accompaniments.

[Example f, f. 18v/p. 34]

---

30. I.e., C major.
31. I.e., D minor.
32. I.e., D minor.
33. In other words, you cannot keep moving from fifth to fifth. You can go from the tonic (D) to the dominant (A) to the supertonic (E), but continuing to the submediant (B) would result in a diminished triad (B, D, F-natural).

Observation

Remarquez qu'au Mode Majeur, on ne va pas tout d'un coup a la Mediante, parce que le semiton, que demande la Mediante altere le ton d'au dessus le mode, qui est re naturel: Car Il faut le diezer, pour cadencer a la Mediante. Mais, au mode mineur, on va tout d'un coup a la mediante sans preparation, parce que Mi, qui est le Ton d'au dessus la finale, est, naturellement, le semiton de la Mediante Fa.

On ne va point aussy de quinte en quinte au mode mineur, parce qu'apres avoir esté de la finale a la Dominante, et de la dominante au Ton d'au dessus le Mode, qui est mi, pour aller de la a la Quinte juste, qui est Si ♮, Il faudroit toucher ce si en nature, ce qui la Modulation du Ton mineur deffend.

f. 18v/p. 34

Il faut donc prendre pour Regle, que, comme au mode majeur la modulation porte a Cadencer de Quinte en Quinte, Au mode mineur la Modulation porte a cadencer de Tierce En Tierce; sans neanmoins, que l'on soit toujours obligé de s'y assujettir.

Des cordes, qui paroissent Equivoques.

On est quelquefois surpris de voir que des basses, dont les nottes semblent les mesmes demandent des accompagnemenᵗ differens.

[Example f, f. 18v/p. 34]

The example shows that the second and third measures contain the same notes as the sixth and seventh. However, one sees by the figures marked above that they need different accompaniments. Knowledge of the notes of the mode removes this difficulty. In the first, second, and third measures, the piece is in A la.[34] Thus La, which is the final, requires a perfect chord. The Sol, which is the whole tone below, needs the sixth. The Fa, which is the sixth of the key, needs the sixth, and Mi, which is the dominant, needs the fifth with a major third. But, in the second example, in the sixth and seventh measures, one is in C ut.[35] Thus C ut needs a perfect chord. The La, which is the sixth of the key, also needs the sixth.

f. 19r/p. 35

The Sol, which is its dominant, needs the fifth. The fourth, Fa, needs the sixth, because one descends by step, and the Mi needs the sixth also, because it is the third or mediant of the key. It is necessary to keep well in mind the notes of the mode when encountering similar occasions.

On Meter and Tempo

Before speaking about dissonances, I believe it is necessary to give a true idea of meter, since without that knowledge one cannot accurately play a bass in a slower tempo, nor put them [dissonances] precisely where they must be. There is scarcely anything that authors have treated less thoroughly, however it seems to me that knowledge about it is highly necessary.

Regarding tempo, one cannot give certain rules with exact precision, because although one puts at the beginning of a work these words—Gravement, Lentement, Gaiement, Vite, Très vite, [or] as the Italians say, Grave, Adagio, Allegro, Presto, Prestissimo—there are still other names, such as Allemande, Gavotte, Sarabande, Menuet, Gigue, Passepied, etc.,

---

34. A minor.
35. C major.

L'exemple fait voir, que les deux et trois*iem*es mesures contienn*ent* les mesmes nottes, que la six*iem*e et la sept*iem*e: Cependant, on voit, par les chiffres marquez au dessus, qu'il leur faut des accompagne-mens differens. La Connoissance des cordes du mode leve cette diffi-culté: Dans les 1. 2. & 3. mesures le chant est en A la: ainsy La, qui est la finale demande l'accord parfait. Le sol, qui est le Ton d'au dessous veut la sixte: le Fa, qui est la sixte de ce Ton veut la sixte, Et mi, qui est la dominante veut la quinte avec la Tierce majeure: Mais, au second exemple des 6. et 7.e mesures, on est en C. ut: Ainsy C ut veut accord parfait. Le la, qui est la sixte de ce Ton veut aussy la sixte.

f. 19r/p. 35

Le sol, qui est sa dominante veut la Quinte: la Quarte Fa veut la sixte a cause, que l'on descend par degrez conjoins, et le Mi veut la sixte aussy, parce qu'il est la Tierce, ou Mediante du Ton: Il faut bien rete-nir les cordes du mode pour de semblables occasions.

De la Mesure, et du Mouvement

Avant de parler des dissonances, Je croy, qu'il faut donner une juste Idée de la mesure, puisque sans la connoistre on ne peut joüer juste Une Basse du moindre mouvement, ny placer precisement dans le lieu, ou ils doivent estre. Il ny a gueres de chose, dont les autheurs ayent moins traité a fonds: cepe*ndant*. Il me semble, que l'Intelligence en est fort necessaire.

A l'egard du mouvement, on ne peut donner de regles certaines dans une exacte precision; Car, quoy qu'on mette au commencement d'un ouvrage ces mots, Gravement, Lentement, gayment, viste, tres viste, comme les Italiens disent, Grave, Adagio, Allegro, Presto, pres-tissimo; Et qu'il y ait encor d'autres noms, comme Allemande, Ga-votte, Sarabande, Menuet, Gigue, passepied, et plusieurs semblables,

whose significance of which is well known among musicians. However, all these names do not always indicate the true character of a piece.

Loulié invented a pendulum, which he called chronometer (in Greek, [the] word means measurement of time), by means of which one can know absolutely the true tempo of the air.

[Marginal note: . .]

In the fifth edition of the *Principes de la musique* of L'Affilard,[36] all the airs are marked at the top of the first page with the chronometer [cord] height, by which the composer has determined the tempo of his air.

This instrument is not, however, appreciated by other authors. To understand the particulars of it, and to see an illustration of it, one can buy the book by Mr. Loulié, which explains it. It is sold at Ballard's, Rue St Jean de Beauvais.[37]

One will also find, in the *Elements de musique* of Loulié, more clarification on the meter signs than in any other, but he did not put them all in. Moreover, it does not cover enough, it seems to me, to impart a complete knowledge of them.

I know that many people recall little of them,

and that it suffices at first for beginners to speak of the most common meters. But there are also curious people whom theory sometimes pleases as much as practice, and it is for them that it is necessary to examine more closely the signs of meter.

It is enough, therefore, in the beginning to know that c is worth four beats, **3** three beats, and two (**2**) two beats.

---

36. Michel L'Affilard, *Principes très faciles pour bien apprendre la musique* (Paris, 1705).

37. Etienne Loulié, *Eléments ou principes de musique, mis dans un nouvel ordre* (Paris, 1696).

f. 19v/p. 36

dont la signification est fort connüe parmy les musiciens, cependant tous ces noms ne marquent pas toujours le vray caractere d'une piece.

Loulié avoit inventé un balancier, qu'il appelloit Kronometre, (mot signifie en Grec mesure du Temps,) par le moyen du quel on pouvoit absolument connoistre le vray mouvement d'un air.

[Marginal note: [ ]ᵉ de [ ]707:⁷]

Dans la cinq*iem*ᵉ Edition des p*rincip*es de la Musique de L'Affilard tous les airs sont marquez au haut de la premiere page du chiffre, que le Kronometre porte a une hauteur certaine, ou le compositeur a determiné le mouvement de son air.

Cet instrument n'est pourtant pas gousté des autres autheurs: Pour en sçavoir les particularitez, et en voir la figure, on peut acheter le livre du sʳ. Loulié, qui en parle: Il se vend ch*ez* Ballard rüe sᵗ. Jean de Beauvais:

On trouvera aussy dans le livre des Elemens de Musique de Loulié, plus d'eclaircissemens sur les signes des Mesures, que dans aucun autre, Mais il ne les a pas tous mis, outre, qu'il ne s'estend pas assez ce me semble, pour en donner la connoissance entiere.

Je sçay, que bien des gens s'en souvient peu,

f. 20r/p. 37

et qu'il suffit d'abord pour les commençans de parler des mesures les plus ordinaires, mais il est aussy des gens curieux, a qui la theorie plaist quelque*fois* autant, que la pratique, et c'est pour eux, qu'il est necessaire d'examiner plus particulierement les signes de la mesure:

Il suffit donc aux commencement de connoistre que le **C**. vaut 4. temps, le **3**. trois temps, et le deux |**2**:| deux temps:

---

7. This leaf is trimmed in such a way as to render the marginal note illegible. It may say something about an edition of 1707. Writer A is probably not referring to Loulié, as his theoretical writings were published in the 1690s. He may be referring to L'Affilard, although the fifth edition of his *Principes*, which is mentioned in the paragraph near the marginal note, was published in 1705.

It is up to the master to demonstrate the way to beat them. The *Traité d'accompagnement* of Saint Lambert speaks of this. ₵ is twice as fast as **C**, $\frac{3}{8}$ is twice as fast as $\frac{3}{4}$, and $\frac{2}{4}$ twice as fast as (**2**).[38]

There are also $\frac{4}{2}$ and $\frac{3}{2}$. $\frac{4}{2}$ marks a meter composed of four half notes in succession, and $\frac{3}{2}$ marks a meter composed of three half notes, or the equivalent, in succession. The tempo of these meters is ordinarily slow.

$\frac{6}{4}$ is composed of two measures of **3**.

$\frac{6}{8}$, of two measures of $\frac{3}{8}$, and is beaten in two equal beats.

$\frac{9}{8}$, of three measures of $\frac{3}{8}$, and is beaten in three equal beats.

f. 20v/p. 38

$\frac{12}{8}$ is composed of four measures of $\frac{3}{8}$ (or, if one will, two measures of $\frac{6}{8}$, because this is the same thing), and is beaten in four equal beats, [with] three eighth notes, or the equivalent, in each beat.

One also finds, in an opera of Lully, a meter of $\frac{4}{8}$. It is beaten in two lively beats. This is "L'Entrée des bergers" in *Roland*, Act 4, Scene 5.[39]

I am going to append examples of all these signs[40] in speaking of the analogy of more specific meters according to different opinions. These are very common in all books that treat the principles of music.

---

38. Saint Lambert's discussion of time signatures is actually found in *Les principes du clavecin*, rather than *Traité d'accompagnement*. He does not include $\frac{2}{4}$ or $\frac{3}{4}$ in the chapter "Des Signes qui Marquent la Mesure et le Mouvement." In a footnote in her translation of this work, Rebecca Harris-Warrick points out that $\frac{2}{4}$ and $\frac{3}{4}$ "were not found in 17th-century French music but were common to Italian music and, in the early 18th century, to Italianate music in France." M. de Saint Lambert, *Principles of the Harpsichord*, trans. Rebecca Harris-Warrick (Cambridge: Cambridge University Press, 1984), 33. See also M. de Saint Lambert, *Les principes du clavecin* (Paris, 1702; repr., Geneva: Minkoff, 1972), 23; M. de Saint Lambert, *Nouveau traité de l'accompagnement du clavecin de l'orgue et des autres instruments* (Paris, 1707; repr., Geneva: Minkoff, 1972).

39. The edition of 1685 does not show a $\frac{4}{8}$ time signature in act 4, scene 5; in act 4, scene 3, there are two instances of $\frac{3}{8}$ time signatures. The first is headed with "Entrée de Pastres, de Pastourelles, de Bergers & de Bergeres," and the second with "Un Pastre, & une Pastourelle, chantent l'Air qui suit." Jean-Baptiste Lully, *Roland* (Paris, 1685; repr., New York: Broude, 2000), 246, 248.

40. See f. 22r/p. 41–f. 22v/p. 42.

C'est au maistre a montrer la maniere de les battre. Le Traité d'accompagnement de S. Lambert en parle. Le $\mathcal{C}$ est une fois plus viste, que le $\mathbf{c}$ ouvert Le $\frac{3}{8}$ est une fois plus viste, que le Triple simple $\frac{3}{4}$, et le $\frac{2}{4}$ une fois plus viste, que le deux Simple |.**2**.|

Il y a encor le quatre double $\frac{4}{2}$ et le Triple double $\frac{3}{2}$. Le quatre double marque une mesure composée de quatre blanches a queüe: Et le Triple double marque une mesure composée de Trois blanches a queüe, ou l'equivalent. Le mouvement de ces mesures est ordinairement lent.

Le $\frac{6}{4}$ est composé de deux mesures a **3**.

Le $\frac{6}{8}$ de Deux mesures a $\frac{3}{8}$ et se bat a 2 temps egaux.

Le $\frac{9}{8}$ de Trois mesures a $\frac{3}{8}$ et se bat a 3. temps egaux.

f. 20 v/p. 38

Le $\frac{12}{8}$ est composé de 4. mesures a $\frac{3}{8}$. (ou si l'on veut de deux mesures a $\frac{6}{8}$. Car c'est la mesme chose) et se bat a quatre temps egaux: Trois croches dans chaque temps, ou l'equivalent

On trouve encor dans un opera de Lully une mesure a $\frac{4}{8}$. Elle se bat a 2. temps legers. c'est. l'entrée des Bergers dans Roland au 4.ᵉ Acte Scene 5.

Je vais Joindre des exemples de tous ces signes, en parlant de l'analogie des mesures plus particuliers. selon les differentes opinions. Ceux cy sont tres communs dans tous les livres, qui Traitent des principes de la Musique.

Observation on the Origin
of All the Meter Signs

That which I have just said can suffice for the early stages. But, to
know the reason why signs were introduced and what enables them
to mark a certain type of meter, it is necessary to point out (as Loulié said in his *Eléments de musique*, third part, page [blank])[41] that
the sign ordinarily consists of two numbers: the one on top is the nu-
merator of the notes and the one on the bottom is the denominator of
the value of the notes; this is to say that the first number shows how
many notes of a certain value the meter will have. This value is determined in relationship to the whole note, which is [notated] in all the
books thus, [example] A.

[Examples A through D, f. 21r/p. 39]

Dividing this note into equal parts according to the first division:
The first division is in two
The second in four
The third in eight
The fourth in sixteen
One knows that two half notes are needed to make the equiva-
lent of the whole note, [example] B. Therefore, the half note is half
of the whole note.

---

41. Etienne Loulié, *Eléments ou principes de musique* (Paris, 1696; repr., Geneva,
Minkoff, 1977), 61.

Observation sur l'origine
de tous les signes de la Mesure

Ce, que Je viens de dire peut suffire dans les commencemens. Mais pour connoistre la raison, qui a Introduit les signes et qui les a determinez chacun en particulier a marquer une certaine Espece d Mesure. Il faut remarquer, (comme Loulier le dit dans ses elemens de Musique 3.ᵉ partie pag*e* [ ]) que le signe est ordinairement marqué par deux chiffres, dont celuy d'au dessus est le numerateur des nottes, et celuy d'au dessous, est le denominateur de la valeur des nottes: c'est a*dire* que le premier chiffre. marque combien la mesure aura des nottes d'une certaine valeur. Cette valeur se determine par rapport a la notte blanche, ou ronde sans queüe, qui est dans tous les livres ainsy A.

[Examples A through D, f. 21r/p. 39]

Divisant cette notte en parties Toujours egales suivant la premiere division

La Premiere division est en deux

La Seconde en quartre

La Troisieme en huit

La Quatrieme en seize

On scait, qu'il faut deux nottes blanches a queüe pour faire l'equivalent de la notte Ronde; B. Donc la notte blanche a queüe est la deuxieme partie de la notte ronde sans queue.

[Marginal note]

One needs four quarter notes to make the equivalent of a whole note, example C. Therefore, the quarter note is the fourth part of the whole note.

Eight eighth notes are needed to make the equivalent of a whole note, [example] D. Therefore, the eighth note is the eighth part of the whole note.

Finally, it takes sixteen sixteenth notes to make the equivalent of the whole note. Therefore, the sixteenth note is the sixteenth part of a whole note.

Let us now examine all the possible meter signs in the following demonstration.

It is necessary to take care that, when the figure which marks the number of beats and that which marks the value of the notes are the same, one only puts one of the two, example [blank].

I want to work [on] a piece in duple time, in which each beat is a half note, which half note is half a whole note. It is evident that it must be marked thus:

[Example g, f. 21v/p. 40]

but that would be pointless. This is the reason why the sign of four beats is alone at the beginning of a piece thus,

[Example h, f. 21v/p. 40]

without a number below, because it shows that it is necessary to beat in four beats, and each beat is a fourth of a whole note, which is a quarter note.

The Italians always mark other kinds of meter with two numbers, [example] E. The French omit [the denominator] in simple triple, thus, [example] F.

[Marginal note[8]]

Il faut 4. noires a queüe pour faire l'equivalant de la Ronde. Exemple: C

Donc la noire a queüe est la quatrieme partie de la Ronde

Il faut 8. croches pour faire l'equivalant de la ronde D.

Donc la croche est la huit*iem*ᵉ partie de la Ronde

Enfin, Il faut seize doubles croches pour faire l'equivalant de la Ronde.

Donc la double croche est la sei*zieme* partie de la Ronde.

Examinons presentement tous les signes possibles de la mesure dans la demonstration suivante.

Il faut prendre garde, que, lorsque le chiffre, qui marque le nombre des temps, et celuy, qui marque la valeur des nottes, sont les mesmes, on ne met, que l'un des deux. Ex.

Je veux travailler une piece a deux temps, dont chaque temps soit une blanche a queüe, la quelle blanche a queüe est un deuxieme de la notte ronde; Il est evident, qu'il les faudroit marquer ainsy

[Example g, f. 21v/p. 40]

Mais cela seroit inutile, Et c'est la raison pouʳ laquelle, le signe a 4. temps, est seul au commencement d'une piece ainsy

[Example h, f. 21v/p. 40]

sans chiffre au dessous, parce qu'il marque, qu'il faut battre a quatre temps, et dans chaque temps un quatrieme de la Ronde, qui est la Noire.

Les Italiens marquent toujours avec autres mesures les deux chiffres: E Les françois l'obmettent au Triple simple ainsy F.

---

8. There are several words in the upper left margin that have been almost completely trimmed away, making it impossible to see what they are.

A l'Italienne
[Italian way]

A la francois
[French way]

[Examples E and F, f. 21v/p. 40]

f. 22r/p. 41

Demonstration of the Meter Signs

A Deux Temps [In two beats]	$\frac{2}{1}$	2	$\frac{2}{4}$	$\frac{2}{8}$	$\frac{2}{16}$
A Trois T. [In three beats]	$\frac{3}{1}$	$\frac{3}{2}$	$\frac{3}{4}$ ou 3	$\frac{3}{8}$	$\frac{3}{16}$
A Quatre T. [In four beats]	$\frac{4}{1}$	$\frac{4}{2}$	c	$\frac{4}{8}$	$\frac{4}{16}$

The first and second sign of each kind are ordinarily slow.
The third, sometimes cheerful, sometimes solemn, the fourth and fifth, almost always very fast.

Demonstration of the Note Values

Tous les signes
derivent de la ronde.
[All the signs
derive from the whole note]

E F

A l'Italienne
[Italian way]

A la francois
[French way]

[Examples E and F, f. 21v/p. 40]

f. 22r/p. 41

Demonstration des signes de la Mesure

A Deux Temps [In two beats]	$\frac{2}{1}$	2	$\frac{2}{4}$	$\frac{2}{8}$	$\frac{2}{16}$
A Trois T. [In three beats]	$\frac{3}{1}$	$\frac{3}{2}$	$\frac{3}{4}$ ou 3	$\frac{3}{8}$	$\frac{3}{16}$
A Quatre T. [In four beats]	$\frac{4}{1}$	$\frac{4}{2}$	c	$\frac{4}{8}$	$\frac{4}{16}$

Les 1.er et le second signe de chaque Espece sont ordinairement Lents.

Le 3. tantost gay, tantost grave le 4. et le 5. presque toujours tres vistes.

Demonstration de la valeur des Nottes.

Tous les signes derivent de la ronde.
[All the signs derive from the whole note]

The other signs are

A deux temps egaux ou a 4. inegaux [In two equal or four unequal beats]	$\frac{6}{4}$	$\frac{6}{8}$	$\frac{6}{16}$
A trois temps [In three beats]	$\frac{9}{4}$	$\frac{9}{8}$	$\frac{9}{16}$
A quatre temps [In four beats]	$\frac{12}{4}$	$\frac{12}{8}$	$\frac{12}{16}$

The first sign of each type is not ordinarily fast, but the last two almost always are.

These last signs are composed of the preceding

Because $\frac{6}{4}$ is made of two measures of $\frac{3}{4}$

$\frac{6}{8}$ of two measures of $\frac{3}{8}$

$\frac{6}{16}$ of two measures of $\frac{3}{16}$,

f. 22v/p. 42

$\frac{9}{4}$ of three measures of $\frac{3}{4}$

$\frac{9}{8}$ of three measures of $\frac{3}{8}$

$\frac{9}{16}$ of three measures of $\frac{3}{16}$

$\frac{12}{4}$ of four measures of $\frac{3}{4}$ or two of $\frac{6}{4}$. Idem.

$\frac{12}{8}$ of four measures of $\frac{3}{8}$ or two of $\frac{6}{8}$. Idem.

$\frac{12}{16}$ of four measures of $\frac{3}{16}$ or two of $\frac{6}{16}$. Idem.

Demonstration[42]

When these first signs [$\frac{6}{4}$, $\frac{9}{4}$, $\frac{12}{4}$?] are marked Allegro or Presto, as often happens, they are beaten as quickly as those which follow them [$\frac{6}{8}$, $\frac{6}{16}$, etc.]. It is necessary to point out, however, that Italian tempos are not as rapid as French tempos.

---

42. The $\frac{12}{16}$ example is erroneously notated with eighth notes in the manuscript.

Les Autres signes sont

A deux temps egaux ou a 4. inegaux [In two equal or four unequal beats]	$\frac{6}{4}$	$\frac{6}{8}$	$\frac{6}{16}$
A trois temps [In three beats]	$\frac{9}{4}$	$\frac{9}{8}$	$\frac{9}{16}$
A quatre temps [In four beats]	$\frac{12}{4}$	$\frac{12}{8}$	$\frac{12}{16}$

Le premier signe de chaque Espece n'est pas viste ordin*ai*^{reme}*nt* mais
les deux derniers le sont presque toujours
Ces derniers signes sont composez des precedens
   Car $\frac{6}{4}$ est composé de deux mesures a $\frac{3}{4}$.
   Le $\frac{6}{8}$ de deux mesures a $\frac{3}{8}$
   Le $\frac{6}{16}$ de deux mesures a $\frac{3}{16}$.

f. 22v/p. 42

   Le $\frac{9}{4}$ de trois mesures a $\frac{3}{4}$.
   Le $\frac{9}{8}$ de trois mesures a $\frac{3}{8}$
   Le $\frac{9}{16}$ de trois mesures a $\frac{3}{16}$
   Le $\frac{12}{4}$ de quatre mesures a $\frac{3}{4}$ ou de deux a $\frac{6}{4}$. id.
   Le $\frac{12}{8}$ de quatre mesures a $\frac{3}{8}$ ou de deux a $\frac{6}{8}$. id.
   Le $\frac{12}{16}$ de quatre mesures a $\frac{3}{16}$. ou de deux a $\frac{6}{16}$. id.

Demonstration

Quand ces premiers signes sont marquez Allegro ou presto,
comme il arrive souvent, Ils se battent aussy viste, que ceux, qui les
suivent. Il faut pourtant remarquer, que les mouvemens Italiens ne
sont pas si precipitez, que les mouvem*ens* francois.

It is still necessary to point out that one finds tempos whose signs are different in the treble and the bass, either at the beginning of the piece or later on, [example] G, and others which seem irregular in the manner in which they are written, [example] H. There are examples of this in the Op. 5 of Corelli, among others [the] third and fourth sonatas,[43] thus.

f. 23r/p. 43

[Examples G and H, f. 23r/p. 43]

Normally, one would find as many notes in the bass as in the treble, or the equivalent. On this occasion, there is a different usage. It is therefore necessary to understand that in these kinds of tempos, three eighth notes [in ¹²⁄₈] do not last longer than one quarter note in the bass, as to the contrary [if the bass were in ¹²⁄₈ and the treble in 𝄵], three eighth notes in the bass do not last longer than one quarter note in the treble, [example] G.

If it should happen that later in the piece one wants to give to the bass as many notes as to the treble, one groups all three together, with a $\overset{\frown}{3}$ and a circle above, as one has seen in example H.

And this is the way to vary the treble or the bass when both have begun with the normal signs in **2**, in **3**, or in **4**. That is common in Italian music.

43. Example G is of the first two measures in the final movement (Allegro) of Corelli's Sonata 3. Example H is measures 5–6 of the final movement (Allegro) of Sonata 4. Both sonatas are found in Arcangelo Corelli, *Sonate a Violino e Violone o Cimbalo, Opus V*, volume 3 of *Historisch-kritische Gesamtausgabe der musikalischen Werke*, ed. Cristina Urchueguia (Laaber, Germany: Laaber-Verlag, 2006), 65, 79.

Il faut encor remarquer, que l'on trouve des mouvemens, dont les signes sont differens du dessus a la basse, soit au commencement de la piece, soit dans la suite de la piece. G. & d'autres, qui paroissent Irreguliers dans la maniere, dont ils sont Ecrits: H Il y en a des exemples Dans le 5.ᵉ œuvre de corelli entrautres Sonate 3.ᵉ & 4.ᵉ Ainsy

f. 23r/p. 43

[Examples G and H, f. 23r/p. 43]

Regulierement, on devroit trouver autant de notes dans la basse, qu'au dessus, ou l'equivalent: En cette occasion, il y a un usage contraire: Il faut donc scavoir, que dans ces sortes de mouvemens, trois croches ne durent pas plus, qu'une noire a la basse, comme au contraire trois croches a la basse ne durent pas plus, qu'une noire au dessus. G.

Que s'il arrive, que dans la suite de la piece on veuille rendre a la basse autant de nottes, qu'au dessus, on les renferme toutes trois ensemble avec un 3̑ et un cercle au dessus, comme on a vû dans l'exemple H.

Et c'est la maniere de diversifier le dessus ou la basse, quand tous les deux ont commencé avec les signes ordinaires a **2**. a **3**. ou a **4**. Cela est commun dans la musique Italienne:

premiere maniere
[first way]

[Example i, f. 23r/p. 43]

autre man.
[another way]

[Example j, f. 23r/p. 43]

Other examples:

f. 23v

There is another way to mark the sign, an example of which is also in the Corelli's Op. 5.

When a piece is marked at first in **c** or in **3** or in $\frac{12}{8}$, and one wants (without taking the trouble to mark the threes with the little circles, as we have just shown) to change the sign from **c** to $\frac{12}{8}$ or from $\frac{3}{4}$ to $\frac{9}{8}$, without changing the tempo, or even from $\frac{12}{8}$ to **c**, thus, [example] J,

[Marginal note: Corelli's Sonata, Op. 5, No. 4][44]

[Example J, f. 23v]

---

44. Example J is of measures 24–29 in the fourth movement (Vivace) of Sonata 4. Arcangelo Corelli, *Sonate a Violino e Violone o Cimbalo, Opus V*, volume 3 of *Historisch-kritische Gesamtausgabe der musikalischen Werke*, ed. Cristina Urchueguia (Laaber, Germany: Laaber-Verlag, 2006), 74.

premiere maniere [first way]

[Example i, f. 23r/p. 43]

autre man. [another way]

[Example j, f. 23r/p. 43]

Autres Exemples.

f. 23v

Il y a encor une maniere de marquer le Signe, dont l'exemple est aussy dans le cinquieme œuvre de Corelli.

Quand une piece est marquée d'abord a **c**. ou a **3**. ou a **¹²⁄₈**., et qu'on veut, (sans se donner la peine de marquer des trois avec de petits cercles, comme nous venons de le demonstrer) changer le signe du **c**. en **¹²⁄₈** ou du **³⁄₄**. en **⁹⁄₈**., sans changer de mouvement, ou bien du **¹²⁄₈** en **c**., ainsy, J

[Marginal note: 4ᵉ Sonate de Corelli: œuvre 5ᵉ]

J.

[Example J, f. 23v]

.. one does it according to example I,[45] where one sees that the treble has nine eighth notes against the value of six in the bass, which the number $\frac{9}{8}$ designates; and to return to the first sign, one puts again six eighth notes instead of nine, which the number $\frac{6}{8}$ indicates in example K.

dans le mesme sonate
[in the same sonata]

[Example K, f. 23v]

In $\mathbf{c}$ or in $\mathbf{2}$ it is the same thing: putting $\frac{12}{8}$ instead of $\mathbf{c}$, and $\frac{8}{12}$ to return to the value of $\mathbf{c}$. Example taken from a cantata by Bononcini:[46]

Chi m'insegna una dona constante

[Example k, f. 23v]

f. 24r/p. 45

The explanation for this is easy. $\mathbf{c}$ is a meter of four quarter notes, and these four quarter notes are worth eight eighth notes.

$\frac{12}{8}$ is also a meter in four, and is similarly beaten in four beats, but it has three eighth notes in each beat, which produces twelve of them in the measure.

Therefore, when the piece is marked with a $\mathbf{c}$ at the beginning, and is subsequently marked $\frac{12}{8}$, the number of eighth notes in each beat increases by a third without changing the tempo, so that this number $\frac{12}{8}$ shows that there are now twelve eighth notes instead of eight.

45. Although not labeled, example I must be the first three measures of example K, f. 23v.

46. According to Lowell Lindgren, this may be a hitherto unknown work by one of the Bononcinis. Lowell Lindgren, email message to this author, January 29, 2011.

On le fait suivant l'exemple I. ou l'on voit que le dessus a neuf croches contre la valeur de six a la basse, ce que le chiffre $\frac{9}{6}$ designe; et pour reprendre le premier signe, on remet six croches au lieu de neuf, ce que le chiffre $\frac{6}{9}$. designe dans l'exemple K

dans le mesme sonate
[in the same sonata]

K.

[Example K, f. 23v]

Au mouvement a **C**. ou a deux c'est la mesme chose: en mettant $\frac{12}{8}$ au lieu du **C**., et $\frac{8}{12}$ pour reprendre la valeur de **C**. Exemple tiré d'une cantate de Bononcini

&c
[etc.]

Chi m'insegna una dona constante

[Example k, f. 23v]

f. 24r/p. 45

L'explication en est facile: Le **C**. est une mesure a quatre noires, et ces quatre noires valent huit croches:

Le $\frac{12}{8}$ est aussy une mesure a quatre, et se bat de mesme a quatre temps, mais il porte trois croches a chaque temps, ce qui en produit douze a la Mesure:

Quand donc la piece est marquée d'un **C**. au commençement, et qu'on marque ensuite $\frac{12}{8}$; le nombre des croches de chaque temps augmente d'un Tiers, sans changer le mouvement: Ensorte, que ce chiffre $\frac{12}{8}$ marque, qu'il y a presentement douze croches, au lieu de huit.

When, on the contrary, from $\frac{12}{8}$ one returns to **c**, which is worth $\frac{8}{12}$, it is to include and reduce the value of three eighth notes to two, so that instead of twelve eighth notes, there will be no more than eight of them: that is, two in each beat, which are the equivalent of a quarter note.

The tempi **2** and **3** are reduced and increased proportionally, as the preceding examples have shown.

The various tempi on which one ordinarily composes are the Allemande, Gavotte, Gigue, Bourrée, Sarabande, Menuet, Passepied, Chaconne, and Passacaille.[47]

f. 24v/p. 46

[blank]

f. 25r/p. 47

On Dissonances

One has seen that there are consonances that want to be followed by other consonances, when the bass ends or rests: these are the fourth and the sixth.

For even better reasons, dissonances need to be followed by consonances, since they are in themselves false chords, and their harshness must be immediately compensated for and reversed by consonances.

I could have spared myself from speaking about them, since they are covered in all books on composition. However, as it has seemed to me that some speak of them too briefly and others not very clearly, I believed it necessary to explain them all in turn and to make known the terms that one uses for them.

---

47. The sense of this is that these dances are the ones composed ordinarily in these tempi.

Quand, au contraire, de $\frac{12}{8}$ on revient au **c**. qui vaut $\frac{8}{12}$ c'est pour comprendre, et reduire la valeur de trois croches en deux, de maniere, qu'au lieu de douze croches, il n'y en aura plus, que huit: scavoir deux dans chaque temps, qui sont l'equivalant d'une noire.

Les mouvements a **2**. et a **3**. se reduisent et s'augmentent de mesme dans leur proportion, comme les exemples precedens l'ont fait voir.

Les differens mouvemens sur lesquels ont[9] Compose ordinaire-men^t sont L'allemande: La Gavotte: La Gigue La bourrée La Sarabande Le Menüet Le passepied La Chaconne: La Passacaille

f. 24v/p. 46

[blank]

f. 25r/p. 47

Des Dissonances.[10]

L'on a vû, qu'il y a des consonances, qui veulent estre suivies d'autres consonances, quand la Basse finit, ou se repose: ce sont la Quarte, et la Sixte.

A plus forte raison les dissonances demandent d'estre suivies des consonances, puisqu'elles sont en elles mesmes de faux accords, et que leur dureté doit estre aussitost reparée, et detruite par des conso-nances.

J'aurois pû me dispenser d'en parler, puisqu'elles sont traitées dans tous les livres de composition: Cependant, comme il m'a parû que les uns en parloient trop en abregé, et les autres peu clairement, J'ay crû, qu'il falloit les expliquer toutes les unes apres les autres, et faire en-tendre les termes, dont on se sert a leur occasion.

---

9. The grammar suggests that this should be *on* instead of *ont*.
10. This is what the Table of Contents calls the Second Part.

It is not only necessary to follow a dissonance with a consonance, which is called "resolving" the dissonance, but also to use it cautiously and with preparation to make it intelligible, which is called "preparing" the dissonance, and to choose for it certain accompanying consonances, when one has made it intelligible, which is called "accompanying" the dissonance.

One also makes use of the words "tie" and "suspension" to mean preparation of a dissonance.

Therefore, one ordinarily says that dissonances must be prepared or tied or suspended. Accompanied. Resolved.

The dissonance is a false interval which is sounded in a treble against the bass, or in the bass against a treble, after one has heard, in a beat of the preceding measure, a consonance on the same degree as that where [the dissonant note] is found.

[Examples A and B, f. 25r/p. 47]

Example A shows that the seventh made by an F in the treble above a G in the bass comes from a perfect fifth on the same degree as the F in the preceding measure on a B-flat in the bass, and this dissonance is tied thus ‾‾‾ above where it is played.

Example B shows the same thing, except that it is the bass which holds, prepares, and resolves a second into a third, which the E of the treble forms against the D of the bass.

Il faut non seulement faire suivre une dissonance d'une consonance, ce qui s'appelle "sauver" la dissonance, mais il faut encor user
de menagement, et de preparation pour la faire entendre, ce qui s'appelle "preparer" la dissonance, et luy choisir certains accompagne-
mens des consonances, lorsqu'on la fait entendre, cequi s'appelle accompagner la dissonance.

On se sert encor du mot de liaison, et de syncope, pour dire, preparation d'une dissonance.

On dit donc ordinairement, que les Dissonances doivent estre,
Preparées, ou Liées, ou Syncopées. Accompagnées: Sauvées.

La Dissonance est un faux accord, qui frappe dans un dessus
contre la basse, ou dans la basse contre un dessus, aprez que l'on a en-
tendu dans un temps de la mesure, qui la precede, une consonance en
mesme degré, que celuy ou elle se trouve pratiquée.

[Examples A and B, f. 25r/p. 47]

L'exemple A fait voir, que la septieme faite par un fa Dans le dessus sur un sol dans la basse vient d'une quinte juste en mesme degré,
qui est pratiquée par le mesme Fa Dans la mesure precedente sur un
Si B. mol de la basse, et cette dissonance est liée ainsy   au dessus, qui la pratique.

L'exemple B. fait voir la mesme chose, si ce n'est que c'est la Basse,
qui tient, qui prepare et qui sauve en tierce une seconde, que le Mi
Du Dessus forme contre le Re De la Basse.

f. 25v/p. 48

Table of the Most Commonly Used Dissonances

[blank staff paper]

f. 26r/p. 49
The ordinary dissonances are divided into perfect and false. Perfect dissonances into major and minor. Perfect dissonances are: 1) the perfect fourth accompanied by the fifth, example D; 2) the second, [example] C; 3) the seventh, [example] E, and 4) the ninth, [example] F.

Major and minor: see the examples.

False dissonances are divided into augmented and diminished.

The augmented dissonances most in use are: 1) the augmented fourth, which one also calls the tritone, [example] G; 2) the augmented fifth, [example] K; and 3) the augmented second, [example] I.

The diminished dissonances most in use are: 1) the diminished fourth, [example] H (this interval is rare); 2) the diminished fifth, [example] L; and 3) the diminished seventh, [example] M.[48]

These last two are common and often combined.

I will speak later of all the other false dissonances that are possible.

An augmented interval is that in which there is a semitone in addition to its perfect value.

A diminished interval is that which has a semitone less than its perfect value. Thus the fourth, which is composed naturally of only two tones and a major semitone, becomes too large by adding another semitone to it, and then one calls it an augmented fourth, or tritone, which means an interval made of three tones. It becomes too small by removing a semitone from its perfect value, and then one calls it a diminished fourth.

---

48. Presumably, examples C through M were to have been on the "Table of the Most Commonly Used Dissonances," on f. 25v/p. 48.

f. 25v/p. 48

Table des dissonances les plus Usitées.

[blank staff paper]

f. 26r/p. 49

Les dissonances ordinaires se divisent en Justes / Fausses.

Les dissonances Justes en Majeures / Mineures.

Les dissonances justes sont: 1. La Quarte Juste accompagnée de la Quinte Ex. D.

2. La seconde C.

3. la Septieme E.

4. La Neuvieme F.

Majeures, et Mineueres: Voyez les Exemples.

Les Dissonances fausses se divisent en Superflües / Diminuées.

Les dissonances superflües les plus en usage sont 1. la Quarte su-
    perflüe, qu'on appelle aussy Triton G.

2. La Quinte superflüe K.

3. La Seconde superflüe I.

Les dissonances diminuées les plus en usage sont 1. La Quarte
    Diminuées H. cet accord est rare.

2. La Quinte diminuée L

3. La Septieme diminuée M.

ces deux derniers sont communs et se joignent souvent
    ensemble.

Je parleray dans la suite de toutes les autres dissonances fausses, qui sont possibles.

Accord superflu est celuy, au quel il y a un Demiton outre sa juste valeur.

Accord diminué est celuy, qui a un Demiton demoins, que sa juste valeur. Ainsy la Quarte, qui n'est composée naturellement, que de deux tons et un demiton majeur, Devient trop grande en y adjou-tant un Demiton de plus, et pour lors on l'appelle quarte superflüe, ou triton, qui veut dire accord composé de trois tons: Elle devient trop petite, en ostant un demiton de sa juste valeur, et alors on l'ap-pelle Quarte diminuée.

Thus the perfect fifth, which must be made up of three tones and a semitone, becomes augmented by adding to it a semitone more, and then it is made up of four tones. It becomes too small by removing a semitone from its perfect value, and then one calls it a diminished fifth, or a false fifth (the latter term is more in use).

The same order applies to dissonances. The second, which is sometimes major and sometimes minor, becomes augmented by adding a semitone. There is no diminished second, and there cannot be one.

The second division of dissonances is [made up] of those which are made in the treble and in the bass.

The second is prepared by the bass. It is the only one that the bass prepares. One has already seen examples of it.

All the other dissonances are therefore made in the treble. It is necessary to explain their accompaniments.

f. 26v/p. 50

Accompaniment of Dissonances

I am convinced that when one has acquired complete knowledge of perfect and imperfect intervals, it will not be difficult to find the accompaniment of the dissonances, since these are the same intervals which one uses to accompany them. It seems to me that this has not yet been said, and that those who have treated dissonances were wrong in not explaining them, since one sees from experience that beginners want to take new ideas when one speaks to them of the accompaniment of dissonances, whereas nothing is simpler when one explains to them that accompaniments of dissonances are those that they already know under the name of perfect and imperfect chords.

[Marginal note: The 2nd]

The natural accompaniment of the major or minor second is the imperfect chord, sixth and fourth. When it is major, one also accompanies it with the augmented fourth, called tritone, and with the major sixth. When it is minor, it is ordinarily the sixth.

Ainsy la Quinte juste, qui doit estre composée de trois tons et un demiton majeur, devient superflüe en luy adjoutant un demiton de plus, et pour lors elle est composée de quatre tons. Elle devient trop petite, en ostant un demiton de sa juste valeur, et alors on l'appelle Quinte diminuée, ou fausse quinte: ce dernier terme est les plus en usage.

Le mesme ordre regne parmy les dissonances: La Seconde, qui est tantost majeure, et tantost mineure devient superflüe en y adjoutant un demiton: Il n'y a point de Seconde diminuée, et il n'y en peut avoir.

La seconde division des dissonances est de celles, qui se font Au Dessus / A la basse.

La seconde est preparée par la basse: c'est la seule, que la basse prepare: on en a deja vû Des Exemples.

Toutes les autres dissonances se pratiquent donc dans le dessus: Il faut expliquer leurs accompagnemens.

f. 26v/p. 50

Accompagnement Des Dissonances.

Je suis persuadé, que quand on aura acquis une entiere connoissance des accords parfaits, et imparfaits, il ne sera pas difficile de trouver l'accompagnement des dissonances, puisque ce sont ces mesmes accors, dont l'on se sert, pour les accompagner. Il me semble, que cela n'a point encor esté dit, et que ceux, qui ont traité des dissonances, n'ont pas eu raison de n'en pas avertir, puisque l'on voit par l'experience, que les commençans veulent prendre des Idées nouvelles, quand on leur parle de l'accompagnement des Dissonances, au lieu, que rien n'est plus simple, quand on leur explique, que les accompagnements des dissonances sont ceux, qu'ils connoissent deja sous le nom d'accors parfaits, et d'accords imparfaits.

[Marginal note: La 2.de]

L'accompagnement naturel de la seconde majeure, ou mineure est l'accord imparfait, sixte, et quarte: Quand elle est majeure on l'accompagne aussy de la quarte superflüe, appelée Triton, et de la sixte majeure: Et quand elle est mineure, la Sixte l'est ordinairement.

One also accompanies the second with the fifth, which one doubles, without adding other consonances. But with respect to this last chord, to me it does not seem very good, because it produces the interval of the third neither against the bass nor between the parts, which is the surest rule for making good harmony.

[Marginal note: The 4th]

The dissonance of a fourth is accompanied by the fifth and the octave. It is a perfect chord without the third.

[Marginal note: The 7th]

The major or minor seventh is added to a perfect chord without removing anything. If one wants to remove something, one removes the octave.

[Marginal note: The 9th]

The major or minor ninth is likewise added to a perfect chord by removing the octave, and one often puts the seventh and the ninth together.

Augmented Intervals

[Marginal note: False 2nd]

The augmented second is accompanied by the tritone and the major sixth. Thus the tritone is accompanied by the major or augmented second and by the major sixth.

[Marginal note: False 4th]

Note that when the bass descends a fourth or ascends a fifth by leap after the tritone, the tritone is accompanied only by the major sixth and the octave. Example

[Marginal note: False 5th]

The augmented fifth is accompanied like a perfect fifth, but it is necessary to suppress the octave, and generally it is joined with the seventh or ninth and even with both together.

On accompagne encor la seconde De la Quinte, que l'on double, sans y joindre d'autre consonance: Mais a l'egard de ce dernier accord, Il ne me paroist gueres bon, parce qu'il ne produit intervalle de tierce ny contre la basse, ny entre les parties, ce qui est la regle la plus sûre pour faire une bonne harmonie.

[Marginal note: La 4.te]

La quarte dissonance est accompagné de la quinte, et de l'octave: c'est l'accord parfait en retranchant la tierce.

[Marginal note: La 7.e]

La septieme majeure, ou mineure entre dans l'accord parfait sans rien retrancher: Et si l'on veut retrancher quelque chose; on retranche l'octave.

[Marginal note: La 9.e]

La neuvieme majeure, ou mineure entre aussi dans l'accord parfait, en retranchant l'octave, et l'on met souvent la 7. et la 9.^e ensemble:

Accords superflus.

[Marginal note: 2.de fausse]

La seconde superflüe s'accompagne du Triton, et de la Sixte majeure Ainsy le Triton s'accompagne de la 2. maj*eu*^re ou superflüe, et de la sixte maj*eu*^re

[Marginal note: 4.te fausse]

Remarquez que quand la basse descend de Quarte, ou monte de Quinte par degrez disjoints apres le Triton, alors le Triton s'accompagne seulement de la sixte majeure, et de l'octave. Ex*ample.*

[Marginal note: 5.te fausse]

La Quinte superflüe s'accompagne comme une quinte juste, mais il faut supprimer l'octave, et communement elle est jointe a la 7.^e ou la 9.^e et mesme a toutes les deux ensemble.

Diminished Intervals

[Marginal note: 4th]

The diminished fourth is accompanied by the sixth and the octave, or by the doubled sixth.

[Marginal note: 5th]

The diminished fifth is accompanied by the sixth and the third.

[Marginal note: 7th]

The diminished seventh is accompanied by the minor third and the false fifth.

f. 27r

Note that when the false fifth is not resolved by the third, and the bass ascends or descends by leap, that is to say apart, one accompanies it like the perfect fifth.

The augmented and diminished intervals are not prepared, if one does not want to, but in addition it is always more agreeable to hear a dissonance prepared by a consonance; it is more secure and more regular to prepare them. One will find them below written in both ways.

After having prepared and accompanied them it is necessary to resolve them, something with which one can never dispense.

The major, minor, and diminished dissonances are all resolved by descending a step after the beat on which one made them. All augmented dissonances are resolved, on the contrary, by ascending. See the examples.

Liberties

Sometimes the seventh is not prepared, as in this example. . . . One also resolves it sometimes with the third by ascending a degree. This is when it is with the ninth and even without the ninth. There are several examples of this in Corelli, when the bass descends by an interval of a third, because on this occasion, the seventh resolved by lowering would produce parallel octaves.

The perfect fifth with the major or minor sixth: although these two consonances seem contrary, on this occasion the fifth is treated like the fourth dissonance, for one prepares it and also resolves it by going down a degree.

Accords Diminüez

[Marginal note: 4.te]

La quarte diminuée s'accompagne de la sixte, et de l'octave, ou de la sixte doublée.

[Marginal note: 5.te]

La quinte diminuée s'accompagne de sixte, et tierce.

[Marginal note: 7.e]

La septieme diminuée s'accompagne de la tierce mineure, et de la fausse Quinte.

f. 27r

Remarquez que quand la fausse quinte n'est pas sauvée de la tierce, et que la basse monte ou descend par degrez disjoints c'est a dire eloignez, on l'accompagne comme la quinte juste.

Les accords superflus et diminüez ne se preparent point, si l'on ne veut, mais, outre, qu'il est toujours plus agreable d'entendre une dissonance preparée par une consonance, il est plus sûr, et plus regulier de les preparer: on les trouvera dans la suite ecrites des deux manieres.

Aprez les avoir preparées, et accompagnées, Il les faut sauver, c'est de quoy l'on ne se dispense jamais.

Les Dissonances majeures, mineures, et diminuées se sauvent toutes en baissant d'un degré aprez le temps, dans le quel on les a faites, et toutes les Dissonances superflües se sauvent au Contraire en montant. Voyez les Exemples

Licences.

Quelquesfois la septieme ne se prepare pas, comme dans cet exemple. . . . On la sauve aussi quelque fois par la Tierce en montant d'un degré: c'est quand elle est avec la 9.e et mesme sans la neuvieme: Il y en a plusieurs exemples dans Corelli, quand la basse descend d'intervalle de tierce, parce que dans cette occasion la septieme sauvée en baissant representeroit deux octaves.

La quinte juste avec la sixte majeure, ou mineure; quoyque ces deux consonances semblent opposées: En cette occasion la quinte est traitée comme la Quarte dissonance, car on la prepare, et on la sauve de mesme en baissant d'un degré.

The major sixth with the false fifth, which produces an augmented second between the parts.

The tritone with the minor third.

Finally, for the convenience of the hands, and to avoid parallel fifths or parallel octaves in the accompaniment, nowadays one uses the sixth with the perfect fourth, or with the tritone, and the third, which some masters call the "little sixth."

One also uses the seventh with the octave and the third, omitting the fifth, or one makes use of the fifth in the same chord and omits the third, according to the position of the hand, it is called the "little seventh."[49]

Dissonances must be prepared, in ¢ or ₵ meter, on the weak beat of the measure (which is [shown] by a rising motion when one beats the meter), made on the strong beat (which is made by a downward motion [in beating time]), and resolved on the weak beat.

The strong beats in ¢ are, therefore, the first and the third, and in ₵ meter, one counts only the first. In ₃ meter, the beats are treated equally, and one can make dissonances on the first, the second, and the third alike.

Note that when one wants to create a dissonance in a treble over a bass note, just watch whether by subsequently going down by step one finds a consonance against the bass on the next beat, for without that it would be badly played.

f. 27v

After having spoken about all the perfect and false dissonances most in use, it is necessary to show now that all the false dissonances can be played according to the talent of the composer, conforming to the expression of certain words, when one composes for the voice.

I will readdress certain dissonances about which I have already spoken, to treat this material more methodically.

---

49. Few authors use this term. Dandrieu and Corrette refer to the seventh respectively as the *Petite Sètième* and the *petite 7.ᵉ* when it is accompanied by the octave and the third. Michel Corrette, *Le maitre de clavecin pour l'accompagnement, methode theorique et pratique* (Paris, 1753; repr., Geneva: Minkoff, 1976), 41–42. Jean-François Dandrieu, *Principes de l'accompagnement du clavecin* (Paris, 1719; repr., Geneva: Minkoff, 1972), 34.

La Sixte majeure avec la fausse quinte, ce qui produit une seconde superflüe entre les parties.

Le Triton avec la tierce mineure.

Enfin pour la comodité des mains, et pour eviter deux quintes, ou deux octaves dans l'accompagnement, on se sert aujourdhuy de la sixte avec la quarte juste, ou ~~superflüe~~ avec le triton, et la tierce: Ce que quelques maistres appellent la petite sixte.

On employe aussy la septieme avec l'octave, et la tierce, en retranchant la quinte, ou l'on se sert de la quinte, dans ce mesme accord, et l'on oste la tierce; selon la position de la main, et l'on l'appelle la petite septieme.

Les Dissonance doivent estre preparées a la mesure de ℂ. ou a **2**. sur le temps foible de la mesure (qui est en levant, lorsqu'on bat la mesure) se faire sur le temps fort, (qui est en frappant,) et se sauver sur le temps foible.

Les Temps forts au grand ℂ sont donc le premier et le troisieme: et a la mesure a **2**, on compte seulement le premier: A la mesure a **3**, les temps sont egaux, et l'on fait des dissonances indifferement sur le 1.er le 2.^{d} et le 3.^{e}

Remarquez, que lorsqu'on veut pratiquer dans un dessus une dissonance sur une notte de basse, il suffit de regarder, si en baissant en suite d'un degré, il se trouve une Consonan^{ce} contre la basse dans la mesure, qui la suit: car sans cela elle seroit mal pratiquée.

f. 27v

Aprez avoir parlé de toutes les dissonances, Justes, et Fausses les plus en usage, Il faut faire voir presentement, que toutes les dissonances fausses se peuvent pratiquer suivant Le genie d'un compositeur, en suivant l'expression de certaines paroles, quand on compose pour des voix.

Je repeteray certaines dissonances, dont j'ay deja parlé, pour traiter cette matiere avec plus d'ordre.

All the False Dissonances Are

I.	II.
Augmented or	Diminished
The second	The third
The third	The fourth
The fourth	The fifth
The fifth	The sixth
The sixth	The seventh
The octave	The octave
There is no augmented seventh. That which is above the major seventh is the perfect octave.	There is no diminished second. That which is below the minor second is the unison.

I have already said that these dissonances are prepared, or not prepared, as one wishes. Here are examples.

The augmented second is accompanied by the tritone and by the major sixth.

f. 28r/f. 1r

XLI. No harmony without a third

[Marginal note: The sixth between the parts takes the place of the third.]

mauvais par deffault de tierce   bon parce [que] la tierce sy trouve
[Bad through absence of a third]   [Good because the third is found]   4 — 3

[Example 1, f. 28r/f. 1r]

This last example shows that the fourth resolved into a third is only a substitution or a suspension of the third.

Toutes les Dissonances Fausses sont

I	II.
Superflües ou	Diminuées
La Seconde	La Tierce
La Tierce	La Quarte
La Quarte	La Quinte
La Quinte	La Sixte
La Sixte	La Septieme
L'octave	L'octave
Il n'y a point de septieme superflüe ce qui est au de la de La septieme majeure, c'est l'octave juste.	Il n'y a point de seconde diminuée ce qui est au dessous de la seconde mineur cest l'unisson.

J'ay deja dit, que ces dissonances se preparent, ou ne se preparent point, si l'on veut: Voici des Exemples:

La seconde superflüe s'accompagne du triton, et de la sixte majeure.

f. 28r/f. 1r

XLI. Point d'harmonie sans tierce.[11]

[Marginal note: la sixte entre les parties tient lieu de la tierce.]

mauvais par deffault de tierce   bon parce [que] la tierce sy trouve
[Bad through absence of a third]   [Good because the third is found]

[Example 1, f. 28r/f. 1r]

Ce dernier exemple montre que la quarte sauvee en tierce n'est q'une supposition ou une suspension de la tierce

---

11. Thus begins the portion of the *Traité* written by Marc-Antoine Charpentier. Many of the numerals in the examples do not appear to be figures, but descriptions of intervals in the chords. Some examples do not exhibit good voice leading and perhaps are not meant to be practical examples.

Perfect intervals 8, 5, and 4 and their replicas[50] are called perfect because they permit neither augmentation nor diminution. Examples:

[Example 2, f. 28r/f. 1r]

Imperfect intervals 6 and 3, major and minor, and their replicas[51] are called imperfect because they do permit augmentation and diminution.

All that goes against variety[52] is a great
mistake in harmony.
That is why two consecutive fifths
of the same type
are forbidden. Examples:

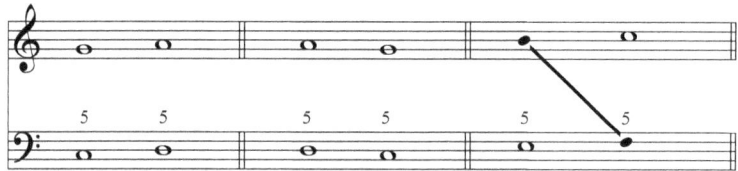

[Example 3, f. 28r/f. 1r]

In this last example there are not only two consecutive fifths, but also a false relation, which is the worst thing in music. I will explain the false relation afterwards.

---

50. I.e., octaves.
51. I.e., octaves.
52. I.e., anything that is monotonous.

acords parfaites 8. 5. et 4 et leurs repliques appellez parfaits parce quils ne souffrent ny augmentation ny diminution Exemples.

[Example 2, f. 28r/f. 1r]

acords imparfaits 6 et 3 maj*eure* et min*eure* et leurs rep*liques* appellez imparfaits parce quils souffrent augmentation et diminution.

> Tout ce qui choque la diversité est une
> grande faute en har[m]onie.
> Cest pourquoy deux quintes de semblable
> espece de suite
> sont deffendues Exemples

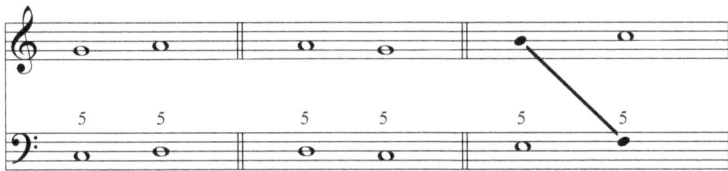

[Example 3, f. 28r/f. 1r]

dans ce dernier exemple il y a non seulement deux quintes de suite mais encore fausse relation c'est ce quil y a de plus mauvais en Musique. J'expliqueray la fausse relation cy après.

On Leading Tones

All notes on which cadences are made have an upper leading tone and a lower leading tone. Examples.[53]

[Example 4, f. 28r/f. 1r]

Minor modes also have a leading tone above their dominants.

The note one chooses for one's mode is called the final. The third above the final is called the mediant, and the fifth above the final is called the dominant.

I have spoken of these leading tones only under the subject of the false relation.

Turn for the following

f. 28v/f. 1v

In Which Sense Two Consecutive Octaves Are Prohibited

The French simply condemn them without considering the accompaniment. Example

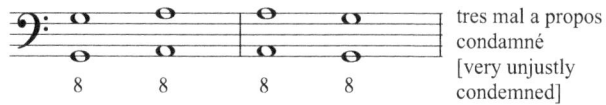

tres mal a propos
condamné
[very unjustly
condemned]

[Example 5, f. 28v/f. 1v]

---

53. In this example, Charpentier uses solmization syllables to show the locations of the upper whole tone and lower semitone described in the text. His mixture of hexachordal syllables and inconsistent use of *si* make the example confusing. For instance, for the first tone, F, he shows the whole tone above as *re*, (G) as solmized in the soft hexachord on F; he shows the semitone below as *si*, which represents a seventh syllable for the seventh scale degree in F. But *si* is also used for the whole step above A three tones later, even though the same pitch is written as *fa♯* when it occurs as the semitone below C. Moreover, toward the end of the example, Charpentier switches to syllables from the natural hexachord, such that a semitone below D is *ut♯*, a whole tone above E is *fa♯*, and so forth.

Des tons et demitons favoris

toutes les notes ou l'on veut faire une cadence ont un ton favori au dessus et un demiton favori au dessous d'elles. Exemples

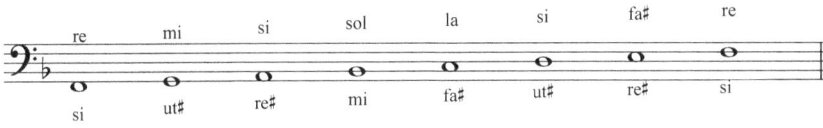

[Example 4, f. 28r/f. 1r]

Les modes mineurs ont encore un demiton favori au dessus de leurs dominantes.

La note qu'on choisit pour son mode s'appelle la finale. La tierce au dessus de la finale s'appelle la mediante et la quinte au dessus de la finale s'appelle la dominante.

Je nay parlé de ces tons et demitons favoris qu'au sujet de la fausse relation.

Tournez pour la suite

f. 28v/f. 1v

En quel sens deux Octaves
de suite sont deffendues

Les François les condamnent simplement sans considerer l'accompagnement Example

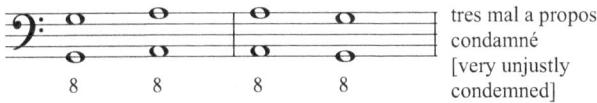

tres mal a propos
condamné
[very unjustly
condemned]

8   8   8   8

[Example 5, f. 28v/f. 1v]

But two consecutive octaves, both accompanied by their third and by their fifth, are prohibited

tres justement
condanné [sic]
[very justly
condemned]

[Example 6, f. 28v/f. 1v]

by the Italians very justly, because these are two consecutive perfect consonances, which go against variety, and all the error comes only from the two consecutive fifths which define the two chords and make them the same type.

Question

When is it that one fears to make two consecutive fifths[?]

[Marginal note: Attention here]

Response

When the bass ascends or descends by step, then it is necessary to play a sixth on the passing note, and a fifth on the stationary note, because the sixth requires something after it, and the fifth requires nothing. This is why the fifth and not the sixth is included in the final chord.

Examples

[Example 7, f. 28v/f. 1v]

Mais deux octaves de suite accompagnees toutes deux de leur tierce
et de leur quinte, sont deffendues

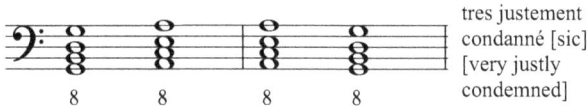

tres justement
condanné [sic]
[very justly
condemned]

[Example 6, f. 28v/f. 1v]

par les Italiens tres justement; parce que ce sont deux consonance[s]
parfaites de suite ce qui choque la diversité, et toute la fau[te] ne vient
que des deux quintes de suite qui determinent les deux accor[ds] et
qui les rendent de semblable espece.

Question

Quand est ce qu'on craint de faire deux quintes de suite

[Marginal note: hic attention]

Reponce

Cest lors que la basse monte ou descend par conjoints, alors il
faut faire sixte sur la note qui ne se repose point, et quinte sur la note
qui se repose parce que la sixte demande quelque chose apres elle, et
la quinte ne demande rien cest pourquoy la quinte entre dans laccord
final et non pas la 6ᵗᵉ

Exemples

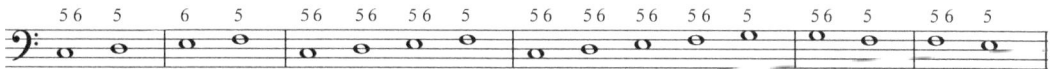

[Example 7, f. 28v/f. 1v]

The Use of
the Third

It is necessary to play a third on the bass where it goes and from where it comes;[54] and also the 5.

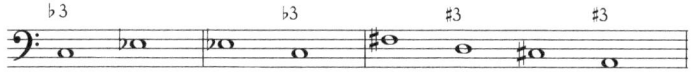

[Example 8, f. 28v/f. 1v]

It is necessary to play a major third on all the dominant [chords] of cadences that one wants to make.

[Example 9, f. 28v/f. 1v]

One ordinarily plays a major third on all the finals. Examples.

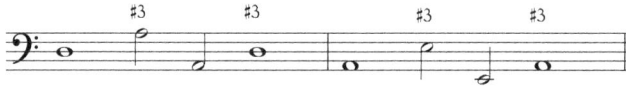

[Example 10, f. 28v/f. 1v]

Notice

The flat lowers a note by a semitone.
The sharp raises a note by a semitone.

---

54. Meaning that the third should be made either major or minor, according to where it is going and from where it is coming.

Pratique
De la Tierce

Il faut faire sur la basse la tierce ou elle va, et d'ou elle vient [&]
aussy la [5].[12]

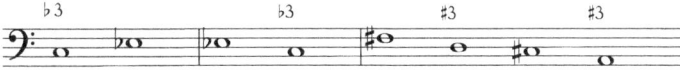

[Example 8, f. 28v/f. 1v]

il faut faire tierce majeure sur toute les dominantes des cadences quon
veut faire

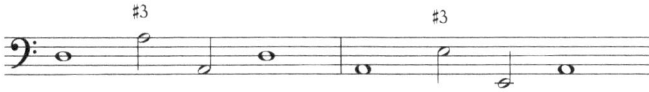

[Example 9, f. 28v/f. 1v]

on fait ordinairement tierce majeure sur toutes les finales Exemples

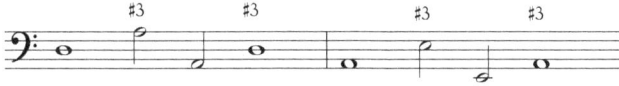

[Example 10, f. 28v/f. 1v]

Remarque

Le b mol donne inclination a baisser apres luy de demiton.
Le ♯ diesis donne inclination a monter apres luy de demiton.

---

12. The "&" and the "5" are essentially illegible, but seem to make sense in the
context.

Use of the Sixth

The major sixth
should always be followed by the octave,
fifth, or third.

Examples

[Example 11, f. 29r/f. 2r]

The Minor Sixth

The minor sixth should always be followed
by the fifth or by the third and never by the
octave unless it is to ascend a step to the
third.

Examples

[Example 12, f. 29r/f. 2r]

One can play as many consecutive sixths and thirds as one wants, because some are major and others minor. Variety is not offended by it.

Any other way of resolving sixths with a third by more distant degrees is rejected.

pratique de la Sixte

La sixte majeure
veut estre toujours suivie de loctave, quinte
ou tierce

exemples

[Example 11, f. 29r/f. 2r]

La sixte mineure

La sixte mineure veut toujours estre suivie
de la quinte ou de la tierce et jamais de
l'octave a moins que ce ne soit pour monter
un degré plus haut
a la tierce

Exemples

[Example 12, f. 29r/f. 2r]

On fait de suite tant de sixtes et de tierces qu'on veut parce que les unes estant majeures et les autres mineures La diversité ny est point choquee

toute autre maniere de sauver les 6.tes ~~par~~ de 3. par degres plus eloignez est rejettée.

Observation

Note that although it is permitted to make several consecutive sixths and thirds, one must nevertheless take care not to make false relations with them.

Proceed to the treatise on the false
relation
Turn

f. 29v/f. 2v

On the False Relation

A false relation is the interval of a tritone or of an augmented fourth which is found between a note of the upper parts, which one has just heard, with a note of the lower parts, which one hears immediately afterwards, and which requires repose.

Examples

[Marginal note: False relations between the treble and the bass]

[Example 13, f. 29v/f. 2v]

In this last example, there are not only false relations, but also parallel fifths.

The fifth is marked on the first note, and the fifth is necessarily implied on the second note, since one rests there.[55]

[Marginal note: False relations between parts]

---

55. As there are no parallel fifths implied in example 13, f. 29v/f. 2v, perhaps Charpentier is referring to example 14, f. 29v/f. 2v.

Observation

remarquez que quoy qu'il soit permis de faire plusieurs sixtes et tierces de suite, on doit neantmoins prendre garde de n'y pas faire de fausse relation.

passez au traité de la fausse
relation
Tournez

f. 29v/f. 2v

De la fausse relation

La fausse relation est lintervalle du triton ou de la quarte super-flue qui se trouve entre une note des parties superieures qu'on vient d'entendre, avec une note des parties inferieures qu'on entend imme-diatement apres et qui demande du repos

Exemples

[Marginal note: fausses relations entre le dessus et la basse]

[Example 13, f. 29v/f. 2v]

dans ce dernier exemple il y a non seulement fausse relation mais en-core il y a deux quintes
la quinte est marquee sur la premiere note et la quinte doit estre sup-posee necessairement sur la seconde note puis qu'on s'y repose.

[Marginal note: fausses relations entre les parties]

[Example 14, f. 29v/f. 2v]

A false relation is that which is worst in music.

Means of Avoiding False Relations

It is to ensure that, by means of a flat or sharp, there is a relation of a perfect fourth instead of a tritone.

[Marginal note: Examples of avoided false relations]

[Example 15, f. 29v/f. 2v]

Remark

One can see by the aforesaid examples that two consecutive major thirds, when the bass descends a tone, create a false relation, but three consecutive major thirds correct it. Examples

[Marginal note: Three consecutive major thirds also correct a false relation.]

[Example 16, f. 29v/f. 2v]

The Si in the treble in fact makes a false relation with the Fa of the bass which comes afterwards, but because the bass does not rest on

[Example 14, f. 29v/f. 2v]

La fausse relation est ce qu'il y a de plus mauvais dans la musique

moyens d'Eviter la fausse relation

Cest de faire en sorte par le moyen du b mol ou du diesis qu'il y ait relation de bonne quarte au lieu de celle du triton

[Marginal note: Exemples des fausses relations Evitées]

[Example 15, f. 29v/f. 2v]

Remarque

on peut remarquer par les sus dits exemples que deux tierces majeures de suite quand la basse descend d'un ton, font fausse re[lation] mais trois tierces majeures de suite la corrigent Exemples

[Marginal note: trois tierces ma*jeure* de suite corrigent aussi la fausse re*lation*]

[Example 16, f. 29v/f. 2v]

the Fa and only rests on the Mi, the false relation is [transformed into] a perfect fifth instead of a tritone.

f. 30r/f. 3r

Application of Leading Tones in False Relations

False relations caused by leading tones not only are permitted, but it is even forbidden to avoid them. Examples in D minor.

[Marginal note: False relations which it is forbidden[56] to avoid]

[Example 17, f. 30r/f. 3r]

Examples in C major

[Marginal note: False relations which it is forbidden to avoid]

[Example 18, f. 30r/f. 3r]

---

56. I.e., impossible.

Le si du dessus a la verité fait fausse relation avec le fa de la basse qui vient apres, mais parce que la basse ne se repose pas sur le fa et quelle ne se repose que sur le mi, la fausse relation et d'une quinte parfaite et non pas de triton.

f. 30r/f. 3r

Application des tons Et demitons
favoris a la fausse relation

Les fausses relations causées par les tons et demitons favoris non seulement sont permises mais il est encore deffendu de les êviter Exemples sur le mode mineur du Ré

[Marginal note: fausses rel*ation* quil est deffendu d'éviter]

demiton favori du re
[leading tone of D]

ton favori du re
[upper leading tone of D]

bonne quarte
[good fourth]

bonne quarte
[good fourth]

belle fausse relation
[beautiful false relation]

belle fausse rel.
[beautiful false relation]

mal evitee
[poorly avoided]

mal evitee
[poorly avoided]

[Example 17, f. 30r/f. 3r]

Exemples sur le mode majeur de l'ut

[Marginal note: fausses relations quil est deffendu d'éviter]

demiton favori de l'ut
[leading tone of C]

ton favori de l'ut
[upper leading tone of C]

bonne quarte
[good fourth]

bonne quarte
[good fourth]

belle fausse rel.
[beautiful false relation]

belle fausse rel.
[beautiful false relation]

mal evitée
[poorly avoided]

mal evitée
[poorly avoided]

[Example 18, f. 30r/f. 3r]

On Dissonances

Dissonances which must be prepared,
tied or suspended and resolved by
descending by step are
ninths, sevenths, and perfect fourths.
There is only one dissonance which must
be prepared and resolved by the bass
descending a step.
It is the second.
The dissonances that are made without being tied, but which need to
    be resolved are:

The diminished or false octave	The augmented octave
The false or diminished fifth	The augmented fifth
The false or diminished fourth	The augmented fourth or tritone
Resolved by descending a step	Resolved by ascending a semitone or a step

Turn
for examples
of all
the dissonances.

f. 30v/f. 3v

Examples of All the Dissonances

[Marginal note: Major and minor ninths and sevenths]

[Example 19, f. 30v/f. 3v]

Des dissonances

Les dissonances qui doivent estre
preparees, liees ou sincopees et sauvées,
par elles mesmes en descendant dun degré,
sont. les neufiemes, septiemes, et quartes parfaites.
Il n'y a q'une dissonance qui doit estre
preparee et sauvee par la basse en
descendant dun degré
C'est la Seconde
Les Dissonances qui se font sans estre liees mais qui veulent estre
    sauvees sont

L'octave diminuee ou fausse,	L'octave superflue
La quinte fausse ou dimin,	La quinte superflue
la quarte fausse ou dimin,	La quarte superflue ou triton
sauvees en baissant d'un degré.	sauvees en Montant de demiton ou d'un degré.

Tournez
pour les Exemples
de toutes
les dissonances.

f. 30v/f. 3v

Exemples de toutes les dissonances

[Marginal note: 9mes et 7mes majeures et min.]

| 9e majeure [major ninth] | 9e min. [minor ninth] | 9e min [minor ninth] | 7e maj. [major seventh] | 7e min [minor seventh] | 7e min [minor seventh] |

[Example 19, f. 30v/f. 3v]

The seventh is also very well resolved into an octave provided that it accompanies the [ninth]. Other than with the ninth it would be badly resolved into an octave.

[Example 20, f. 30v/f. 3v]

When the bass ascends in fourths and descends in fifths, one can play a seventh on all the notes that touch these degrees.

[Marginal note: Major and minor seconds]

[Example 21, f. 30v/f. 3v]

Of the Fourth

Although the fourth is a perfect consonance, one sometimes considers it as a dissonance and sometimes as a consonance.

La septieme est encore fort bien sauvee en octave pour veu quelle accompagne la Septieme[13] autrement qu'avec la neufieme elle seroit mal sauvee en 8

[Example 20, f. 30v/f. 3v]

quand la basse monte de quartes et descend de quinte[s] on peut faire 7ᵉ sur toutes les nottes qui touchent ces degres

[Marginal note: Secondes majeures et min.]

[Example 21, f. 30v/f. 3v]

De la Quarte

Quoyque la Quarte soit une consonance parfaite on la considere quelques fois comme dissonance et quelque fois comm[e] Comme Consonance

---

13. This seems to be a redundant *septième*. He must mean *neuvième*.

The Fourth Considered
as a Dissonance

Under the final of the mode 8
Under the leading tone above 5
Under the leading tone below 3♯
Under the sixth in the minor mode 3♭
And under the mediant 3
And under the dominant 5

[Marginal note: The fourth considered as a dissonance is prepared the same and is resolved the same in descending by step, like the ninth and seventh.]⁵⁷

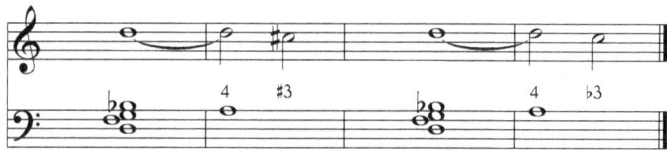

[Example 22, f. 30v/f. 3v]

f. 31r/f. 4r

The Fourth Considered
as a Consonance

The fourth considered as a consonance is played between the parts without being tied or resolved. Against the bass, it is not prepared if one does not want, but it always resolves to a sixth by ascending a step. Examples⁵⁸

57. This example must be meant for explanatory purposes and not for actual practice. It may be that the inner notes are alternative choices: either a 6/4 or a 6/3 chord.

58. The numerals in this and many of the examples to follow appear to be descriptive of intervals found in the chords rather than figured bass.

Quarte consideree
Comme dissonance

Sous la finale du mode 8.

s*ous* le ton favori d'audessus 5.

s*ous* le ton favori d'audessous 3♯

s*ous* la 6te au mode min. 3.♭

et sous la mediante 3.

et s*ous* la dominante la 5.

[Marginal note: La quarte consi*d*eree comme disson*ance* se prepare elle mesme et se sauve elle mesme en baissant dun degré comme la 9e et 7e]

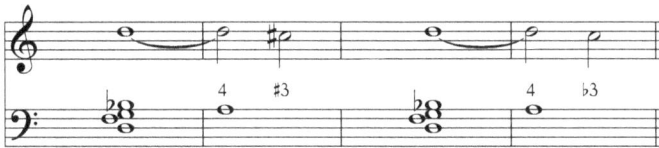

[Example 22, f. 30v/f. 3v]

f. 31r/f. 4r

Quarte Consideree
Comme Consonance

La Quarte consideree comme consonance se pratique entre les parties sans estre liee ny sauvee. ~~mais~~ et contre la basse, elle ne se prepare point si lon ne veut mais elle se sauve toujours en sixte en montant dun degré. Exemples

commencement [beginning]   fin [end]

[Example 23, f. 31r/f. 4r]

General Rules
for Ninths, Sevenths, Fourths, and Seconds

These four dissonances are always prepared on a weak beat, are made on a strong beat, and are resolved on a weak beat. See the examples above.

These same four dissonances are also played on a held bass note, are made on weak notes,[59] and are resolved on strong notes by progressing by step to the nearest consonance, both ascending and descending. Examples

[Example 24, f. 31f/f. 4r]

Turn for
the continuation of the treatise on
the fourth.

---

59. I.e., beats.

commencement [beginning]   fin [end]

[Example 23, f. 31r/f. 4r]

Reigles generales
Pour les 9^{es} 7^{es} 4^{es} et 2des

Ces quatre dissonances se preparent toujours sur un temps foible, se font sur un temps fort, et se sauvent sur un temps foible. voyez les exemples cy devant.

Ces quatre mesmes dissonances se pratiquent encore sur une tenüe de basse, se font sur les notes foibles et se sauvent sur les notes fortes en cheminant de degré conjoint sur la consonance la plus proche tant en montant quen descendant. Exemples

[Example 24, f. 31f/f. 4r]

Tournez pour
la suite du traité de
la Quarte.

Several Consecutive Fourths
[Are] Permitted between Parts and
against the Bass Provided That between
All These Fourths There Is One of a
Different Type

Examples

[Marginal note: Several consecutive fourths between parts],

[Example 25, f. 31v/f. 4v]

and as the fourth is an inverted fifth, several consecutive fifths between parts and even against the bass are similarly allowed.

Examples

[Marginal note: Several consecutive fifths between parts]

[Example 26, f. 31v/f. 4v]

f. 31r/f. 4v

Plusieurs Quartes de suite
Permises entre les parties Et
Contre la basse
Pourveu qu'entre toutes ces quartes il y en
ait quelque une de differente espece

Exemples

[Marginal note: plusieurs 4.ᵉˢ de suite entre les parties]

[Example 25, f. 31v/f. 4v]

et comme la Quarte est une Quinte renversee plusieurs Quintes entre les parties et mesme contre la basse sont pareillem[ent] permises de suite.

Exemples

[Marginal note: plusieurs quintes de suite entre les parties]

[Example 26, f. 31v/f. 4v]

[Marginal note: Two consecutive fourths and not more against the bass]

[Example 27, f. 31v/f. 4v][60]

These last two examples demonstrate the effectiveness of the third between the parts when not made with the bass.

[Marginal note: [Two] consecutive fifths but no more against the bass. One perfect, and one diminished.]

[Example 28, f. 31v/f. 4v]

Examples of dissonances which are not tied if one does not want, but which need to be resolved by descending a step

[Marginal note: Diminished dissonances]

octave diminuee seulement de ces deux manieres [diminished octave [used] only in these two ways]

Quinte diminuee ou fausse [diminished or false fifth]

quarte dimin. seulement de cette maniere [diminished fourth [used] only in this way]

[Example 29, f. 31v/f. 4v]

---

60. The numerals in the third measure appear to be describing intervals, but the 9♯ does not fit this explanation. Perhaps it is meant to be a 4♯, and the subsequent 9 a 4. If the chords in these two measures were figured, the functional progression would be as follows: root position, 6/4♯/2, 6/4/2, cadence.

[Marginal note: Deux 4.es et pas plus contre la basse, de suite]

[Example 27, f. 31v/f. 4v][60]

ces deux derniers exemples prouvent lefficace de la tierce entre les
parties quand on ne la fait pas avec la basse

[Marginal note: [Deux] 5tes de suite mais pas plus avec la basse. [U]
ne juste, Et [un]e diminués

[Example 28, f. 31v/f. 4v]

Exemples des dissonances qui ne se lient point si lon ne veut mais
qui veulent estre sauvees un degré plus bas

[Marginal note: [D]issonances [d]imin*ués*]

octave diminuee seulement
de ces deux manieres
[diminished octave [used]
only in these two ways]

Quinte diminuee ou fausse
[diminished or false fifth]

quarte dimin. seulement de
cette maniere
[diminished fourth [used]
only in this way]

[Example 29, f. 31v/f. 4v]

f. 32r/f. 5r

Examples of dissonances which are not tied if one does not want, but which need to be resolved by ascending a step

[Marginal note: Augmented dissonances]

Octave superf
seulement de
cette maniere
[augmented octave
only in this way]

Quinte superflue
[augmented fifth]

Quarte superf
ou triton
[augmented fourth
of tritone]

[Example 30, 32r/f. 5r]

The Practice of Consonances in Summary

Do not move from perfect to perfect by similar motion because that goes against variety.

Examples

[Marginal note: From perfect interval to perfect]

mauvais [bad]

[Example 31, f. 32r/f. 5r]

One is able to do this, provided that the treble progresses by step and that the bass leaps by fourth or fifth.

f. 32r/f. 5r

Exemples des dissonances Qui ne se lient point si lon ne veut,
mais qui veulent estre sauvees un degré plus haut

[Marginal note: dissonances superflues]

Octave superf
seulement de
cette maniere
[augmented octave
only in this way]

Quinte superflue
[augmented fifth]

Quarte superf
ou triton
[augmented fourth
of tritone]

[Example 30, 32r/f. 5r]

Pratique des Consonances
en abregé

ne passez point du parfait au parfait par mouvement semblab[l]
e parce que la diversité y est choquee

Exemples

[Marginal note: de l'accord parfait au parfait]

mauvais [bad]

[Example 31, f. 32r/f. 5r]

cvon le peut faire pour veu que le dessus chemine de degré
conjoint et que la basse saute de 4 ou 5

bon [good]   meilleur [better]   permis a 4 parties
                                           seulement
                                           [permitted in
                                           four parts only]

[Example 32, f. 32r/f. 5r]

Do not move from imperfect to perfect by similar motion, because there is an offense against variety, for not only are two consecutive fifths and two octaves errors, but also all that which resembles them.

Examples

[Marginal note: From the imperfect interval to the perfect]

la sixte est outre cela mal
sauvée en 8.ve de cette maniere
[The sixth is, besides that, badly
resolved into octaves in this manner.]

cela ressemble   cela ressem
a deux octaves et   a deux
la sixte n'est   quintes
pas sauvee   [this resembles
comme il faut   parallel
[this resembles   fifths]
parallel octaves and
the sixth is
not resolved properly]

[Example 33, f. 32r/f. 5r]

bon [good]   meilleur [better]   permis a 4 parties
                                               seuleme*n*t
                                               [permitted in
                                               four parts only]

[Example 32, f. 32r/f. 5r]

Ne passez point non plus de l'imparfait au parfait par mouvement semblable parce [que] la diversité y est choquee car non seulement deux 5tes et 2 8mes de suite sont des fautes mais aussi tout ce qui
leur ressemble

Exemples

[Marginal note: de l'accord imparf au parfait]

la sixte est outre cela mal
sauvée en 8.ve de cette maniere
[The sixth is, besides that, badly
resolved into octaves in this manner.]

cela ressemble   cela ressem
a deux octaves et   a deux
la sixte n'est   quintes
pas sauvee   [this resembles
comme il faut   parallel
[this resembles   fifths]
parallel octaves and
the sixth is
not resolved properly]

[Example 33, f. 32r/f. 5r]

bon [good]   meilleur [better]

[Example 34, f. 32r/f. 5r]

One can do this provided that the treble moves by step and that the bass leaps by fourth or fifth.

Turn for the
Continuation.

f. 32v/f. 5v

Of the Fugue

The fugue is the imitation of the subject at the fourth or fifth above or below; sometimes at the octave and the unison.

[Example 34, f. 32r/f. 5r]

on le peut faire pour veu que le dessus chemine par degre conjoint et que la basse saute de quarte ou de quinte

Tournez p*our* la
suite.

f. 32v/f. 5v

De la Fugue

La fugue est la representation de chant a la quarte ou a la quinte au dessus ou au dessous quelque fois a l'octave et a l'unisson

Examples

fugue a la quarte au dessus [fugue at the fourth above]

fugue a la quinte au dessous [fugue at the fifth below

fugue a Loctave moins belle que les deux autres [fugue at the octave; less beautiful than the two others]

second dessein [countersubject]

fugue a Lunisson pas plus belle qu'a l'octave [fugue at the unison; less beautiful than at the octave]

[Example 35, f. 32v/f. 5v]

Exemples

fugue a
la quarte
au dessus
[fugue at
the fourth
above]

fugue a
la quinte
au dessous
[fugue at
the fifth
below

fugue a
Loctave
moins belle
que les deux
autres [fugue at
the octave;
less beautiful
than the two
others]

second dessein [countersubject]

fugue a
Lunisson
pas plus belle
qu'a l'octave
[fugue at
the unison;
less beautiful
than at the octave]

[Example 35, f. 32v/f. 5v]

Remarks to Gladden the Disciple

Note that the third is the most beautiful of all intervals because of its small size and of the ease with which the mind can grasp it. The sixth goes after the third, because of its usefulness for avoiding two consecutive fifths. Furthermore, the sixth is an inverted third, and inverted objects, like a tree seen in water, are not as beautiful as those seen in their true orientation. Nevertheless, the sixth between parts takes the place of the third, and this is not without reason, because beautiful inverted objects, in my opinion, are worth as much as those that are on their feet.[61]

f. 33r/f. 6r

Continuation

The first in beauty, therefore, is the third, the second is the sixth, the third is the fifth, after the fifth it is the octave, and the least of all the intervals is the unison.

On Imitation

Imitation is the reiteration of a little melody at the second, at the third, or at the unison. Example

[Marginal note: Imitation must not be as long as a fugue.]

a lunisson [at the unison]   a la seconde [at the second]

[Example 36, f. 33r/f. 6r]

---

61. I.e., the right way up.

Remarque pour esgayer le disciple

remarquez que la tierce est le plus beau de tous les accords a cause de son peu dEstendue et de la facilité. qu'a l'esprit a la concevoir. La sixte marche apres la tierce, a cause de l'utilité de sa pratique pour eviter deux quintes de suite. de plus la sixte est une tierce renversee, et les objets renversez, comme un arbre veu dans l'eau, ne sont/nest[14] pas si beaux que veus dans leurs sens. neantmoins la sixte entre les parties, tient lieu de la tierce, et ce nest pas sans raison car les beaux objets renversez, a mon avis, vallent bien ceux qui sont sur leurs pieds.

f. 33r/f. 6r

Suite

La premiere donc en beauté, c'est la tierce, la seconde c'est la sixte, la troisieme c'est la quinte, apres le Quinte c'est lOctave, et le moindre de tous les accords c'est l'unisson.

De Limitation

L'imitation est la representation dun petit chant a la seconde a la Tierce ou a lunisson. Exemple

[Marginal note: l'imitation ne doit pas estre si longue que la fugue]

[Example 36, f. 33r/f. 6r]

---

14. In the manuscript, "ne sont" is written in above "nest."

Note

. . . that imitation can be practiced only in like voices, because bass voices cannot approach high voices so closely that they can take their unisons, seconds, or even thirds without being extremely forced and without covering them. This is a bad effect made by French composers who raise their basses so high that although their compositions are in four, five, and six parts, it seems that they have composed only in one, because one only hears the basses.

The way of guarding against this disadvantage is to put all the voices in their own tessitura and not to force the range of any of them.

voix [voices]

haut dessus	bas dessus	haute contre	haute Taille	basse Taille	concordant	basse contre
[high treble]	[low treble]	[high tenor]	[tenor]	[baritone]	[bass]	[low bass]

Instr. [Instruments]

dessus de violon	flute a bec	flute allem.	haute Contre de violon	Taille de violon	quinte de violon	basse de violon
[treble violin]	[recorder]	[transverse flute]	[countertenor violin]	[tenor violin]	[fifth violin]	[bass violin]

on peut faire aller ces trois parties plus haut ou plus bas. mais plus haut elles sont aigres et criardes et plus bas elles sont confondües dans les basses.
[One can make these three parts go higher or lower, but higher they are sour and shrill and lower they are confused in the basses.]

[Example 37, f. 33r/f. 6r]

Remarquez

Que l'imitation ne se peut pratiquer qu'à voix pareilles parce que les voix basses ne peuvent approcher de si pres les aigües quelles puissent prendre leurs unissons, leurs secondes ny mesme leurs tierces sans estre extremement forcees et sans les couvrir cest le mauvais effet que font les compositeurs a la françoise qui guindent leurs basses si haut, que bien que leurs compositions soient a 4 5 et six parties il semble quils n'ayent composé qua un parce qu'on nentend que les basses.

Le Moyen d'obvier a Cet inconvenient cest de mettre toutes les Voix dans leur Diapazon et de n'en forcer aucune Estendue des voix.

voix [voices]						
haut dessus [high treble]	bas dessus [low treble]	haute contre [high tenor]	haute Taille [tenor]	basse Taille [baritone]	concordant [bass]	basse contre [low bass]

Instr. [Instruments]						
dessus de violon [treble violin]	flute a bec [recorder]	flute allem. [transverse flute]	haute Contre de violon [countertenor violin]	Taille de violon [tenor violin]	quinte de violon [fifth violin]	basse de violon [bass violin]

on peut faire aller ces trois parties plus haut ou plus bas.
mais plus haut elles sont aigres et criardes et plus bas
elles sont confondües dans les basses.
[One can make these three parts go higher or lower,
but higher they are sour and shrill and lower
they are confused in the basses.]

[Example 37, f. 33r/f. 6r]

Summary

Play a third against the bass or between the other parts, otherwise [there is] no harmony.

Play a sixth when the bass progresses by step, and resolve the sixth into an octave, fifth, or third.

Observe contrary motion between the parts against the bass.

Make no false relation which is not caused by the leading tones of the cadence where you want to land.

Finally, so that variety is never offended, neither actually [move] by consecutive perfect intervals nor by that which resembles them, and you will make perfect music.

This example shows the plan it is necessary to form in making the bass under a treble.[62]

[Example 38, f. 33v/f. 6v]

62. Example 38, f. 33v/f. 6v, is squeezed in between the end of the previous line and the *Fin.* Also note that the text above the staff is vertical in the manuscript.

f. 33v/f. 6v

Recapitulation

faites tierce contre la basse ou entre les parties autrement point
   d'harmonie.

Faites sixte quand la basse chemine par degres conjoints et sau-
   vez la sixte en octave quinte ou tierce

Observez le mouvement contraire entre les parties contre la
   basse.

ne faites aucune fausse relation qui ne soit causees par les tons ou
   demitons favoris de la cadence ou vous voulez tomber.

Enfin que la diversité ne soit jamais choquee ny effectivement
   par les accords parfaits de suite ny par ce qui leur ressemble et
   vous ferez de la musique parfaite

Cet exemple montre le dessein quil faut former En faisant la
   basse sous un dessus:

[Example 38, f. 33v/f. 6v]

End

One doubles major thirds less than the others.

The cadence on the fifth is [like] the period . in speech.

In $\frac{6}{4}$, [there are] two quarter notes in the first beat [of the hand], one in the second, two in the third, and one in the fourth.

Fin

On double moins les tierces maj*eures* que les aut*res*.[15]

La cadence de quinte; est le poinct . dans le discours

a $\frac{6}{4}$ deux noires dans le premier temps une dans la deux*iem*ᵉ deux dans le 3.ᵉ une dans le 4.ᵉ

---

15. This and the final paragraph are written in lighter ink than the surrounding writing and appear to be in a third hand (neither Writer A nor Charpentier).

Bibliography

Seventeenth- and Eighteenth-Century Sources

Agazzari, Agostino. *Del sonare sopra'l basso con tutti li stromenti e dell'uso loro nel concerto*. Siena, 1607. Reprint, Bologna: Forni, 1969.

Bianciardi, Francesco. *Breve regola para imparar'a sonare sul Basso*. Siena, 1607. In *Œuvres théoriques completes. Ars musices iuxta consignationes variorum scriptorum. Renaissance et période préclassique. Domaine Italien 1*. Paris: Editions du Cerf, 1996.

Brossard, Sebastien de. *Dictionnaire de musique, contenant une explication des termes Grecs, Latins, Italiens, & François, les plus usitez dans la musique*, 2nd ed. Paris, 1705. Reprint, Hilversum, Netherlands: Frits Knuf, 1965.

Campion, François. *Traité d'accompagnement et de composition selon la règle des octaves de musique; Addition au Traité d'accompagnement par la règle d'octave*. Paris, 1716; 1730. Reprint, Geneva: Minkoff, 1975.

Charpentier, Marc-Antoine. *Œuvres complètes*. Part 1, *Meslanges autographes*. Paris: Minkoff, 2004.

Corelli, Arcangelo. *Sonate a Violino e Violone o Cimbalo, Opus V. Historisch-kritische Gesamtausgabe der musikalischen Werke*, III. Edited by Cristina Urchueguia. Laaber, Germany: Laaber-Verlag, 2006.

Corrette, Michel. *Le maitre de clavecin pour l'accompagnement, methode theorique et pratique*. Paris, 1753. Reprint, Geneva: Minkoff, 1976. English translation as *Le maître de clavecin pour l'accompagnement: Michel Corrette's Method for Learning to Accompany from a Thoroughbass; a Translation and Commentary*. Translated by Gordon S. Rowley. Iowa City: University of Iowa, 1979.

Couperin, François. *Les Goûts-réünis ou Nouveaux Concerts*. Paris, 1724. Edited by André Schaeffner. Reviewed according to the sources by Kenneth Gilbert and Davitt Maroney. Monaco: Editions de l'Oiseau-Lyre, 1988.

Dandrieu, Jean-François. *Principes de l'accompagnement du clavecin*. Paris, 1719. Reprint, Geneva: Minkoff, 1972.

d'Anglebert, Jean Henry. *Pièces de clavecin*. Paris, 1689. Reprint, Geneva: Editions Minkoff, 2001. Edited by Kenneth Gilbert. Paris: Heugel, 1975.

Delair, Denis. *Nouveau traité d'accompagnement pour le theorbe, et le clavessin*. Paris, 1724. Reprint in *Basse continue: France 1600–1800:*

Methodes, traites, ouvrages generaux, prefaces, periodiques, v.
2, compiled by Jean Saint-Arroman, 145–94. Courlay: Editions
Fuzeau, 2006. English translation as *Accompaniment on Theorbo
and Harpsichord: Denis Delair's Treatise of 1690: A Translation and
Commentary by Charlotte Mattax*. Bloomington: Indiana University Press, 1991.

———. *Traité d'accompagnement pour le théorbe et le clavecin*. Paris, 1690.
Reprint, Geneva: Minkoff Reprint, 1972.

Dictionnaire de l'Académie française, 1st ed. (1694). In the ARTFL Project.
http://artfl-project.uchicago.edu/content/dictionnaires-dautrefois.

Furetière, Antoine. *Dictionnaire de musique d'après Furetière: 1690*. Béziers:
Société de musicologie de Languedoc, 1987.

Gasparini, Francesco. *L'Armonico pratico al cimbalo*. Venice, 1708. Reprint,
New York: Broude, 1967. English translation as *The Practical Har-
monist at the Harpsichord*. Translated by Frank S. Stillings. New
Haven: Yale University Press, 1963.

L'Affilard, Michel. *Principes très faciles pour bien apprendre la musique*.
Paris, 1705. Reprint, Geneva: Minkoff, 1979.

Loulié, Etienne. *Eléments ou principes de musique, mis dans un nouvel ordre*. Paris, 1696. Reprint, Geneva: Minkoff, 1971. English translation
as *Elements or Principles of Music*. Paris, 1696. Translated by Albert
Cohen. New York: Institute of Mediaeval Music, 1965.

Lully, Jean-Baptiste. *Roland: Tragédie en musique*. Paris, 1685. Reprint,
New York: Broude, 2000.

Masson, Charles. *Nouveau traité des règles pour la composition de la musique*. Paris, 1699. Reprint, New York: Da Capo Press, 1967.

Mersenne, Marin. *Harmonie universelle: contenant la théorie et la pratique
de la musique*. Paris, 1636. Reprint, Paris: Éditions du Centre Na-
tional de la Recherche Scientifique, 1965.

Nivers, Guillaume Gabriel. *L'Art d'accompagner sur la basse continue pour
l'orgue et le clavecin*. Paris, 1689. Reprint, Geneva: Minkoff, 2000.

———. *Traité de la composition de musique*. Paris, 1667. English translation
as *Treatise on the Composition of Music*. Translated and edited by
Albert Cohen. Brooklyn: Institute of Mediaeval Music, 1961.

Rousseau, Jean. *Méthode claire, certaine et facile pour apprendre à chanter
la musique*. Paris, 1691. Translated by Robert A. Green as *A Clear,
Sure, and Easy Method for Learning to Sing*, in his "Annotated
Translation and Commentary of the Works of Jean Rousseau: A
Study of Late Seventeenth-Century Musical Thought and Perfor-
mance Practice." PhD diss., Indiana University, 1979.

Saint Lambert, M. de. *Nouveau traité de l'accompagnement du clavecin de l'orgue et des autres instruments*. Paris, 1707. Reprint, Geneva: Minkoff, 1972. English translation as *A New Treatise on*

Accompaniment with the Harpsichord, the Organ, and with Other Instruments. Translated and edited by John S. Powell. Bloomington: Indiana University Press, 1991.

———. *Les principes du clavecin*. Paris, 1702. Reprint, Geneva: Minkoff, 1972. English translation as *Principles of the Harpsichord*. Translated by Rebecca Harris-Warrick. Cambridge: Cambridge University Press, 1984.

Twentieth- and Twenty-First-Century Sources

Barnett, Gregory. "Tonal Organization in Seventeenth-century Music Theory." In *The Cambridge History of Western Music Theory*, edited by Thomas Christensen, 407–55. Cambridge: Cambridge University Press, 2002.

Cessac, Catherine. *Marc-Antoine Charpentier*. Paris: Fayard, 1988. English translation as *Marc-Antoine Charpentier*. Translated by E. Thomas Glasow. Portland, OR: Amadeus Press, 1995.

Christensen, Jesper Bøje. *18th Century Continuo Playing: A Historical Guide to the Basics*. Translated by J. Bradford Robinson. Kassel: Bärenreiter, 2002.

Christensen, Thomas. *Rameau and Musical Thought in the Enlightenment*. Cambridge: Cambridge University Press, 1993.

———, et al. *Towards Tonality: Aspects of Baroque Music Theory*. Leuven: Leuven University Press, 2007.

Cohen, Albert. *Music in the French Royal Academy of Sciences: A Study in the Evolution of Musical Thought*. Princeton, NJ: Princeton University Press, 1981.

———. "'La Supposition' and the Changing Concept of Dissonance in Baroque Theory." *Journal of the American Musicological Society* 24, no. 1 (spring 1971): 63–84.

Gaudriault, Raymond. *Filigranes et autres caractéristiques des papiers fabriqués en France aux XVIIᵉ et XVIIIᵉ siècles*. Paris: CNRS Editions, 1995.

Gosine, C. Jane. "Questions of Chronology in Marc-Antoine Charpentier's Meslanges Autographes: An Examination of Handwriting Styles." *Journal of Seventeenth-Century Music* 12, no. 1 (2006). Accessed January 14, 2019. https://sscm-jscm.org/v12/no1/gosine.html.

Heawood, Edward. *Watermarks Mainly of the 17th and 18th Centuries*. Hilversum, Holland: Paper Publications Society, 1986.

Hitchcock, H. Wiley. *Marc-Antoine Charpentier*. Oxford: Oxford University Press, 1990.

———. *Les œuvres de Marc-Antoine Charpentier: catalogue raisonné.* Paris: Picard, 1982.

Lester, Joel. *Compositional Theory in the Eighteenth Century.* Cambridge, MA: Harvard University Press, 1992.

Palisca, Claude. *Music and Ideas in the Sixteenth and Seventeenth Centuries.* Urbana: University of Illinois Press, 2006.

Ranum, Patricia M. *Vers une chronologie des œuvres de Marc-Antoine Charpentier: les papiers employés par le compositeur: un outil pour l'étude de sa production et de sa vie.* Baltimore: author, 1994.

Thompson, Shirley. "Reflections on Four Charpentier Chronologies." *Journal of Seventeenth-Century Music* 7, no. 1 (2001). Accessed January 14, 2019. http://sscm-jscm.org/v7/no1/thompson.html.

Zappulla, Robert. *Figured Bass Accompaniment in France.* Turnhout: Brepols, 2000.

Index

Page numbers in italics refer to illustrations.

CARLA E. WILLIAMS is Music and Special Projects
Librarian for the Ohio University Libraries.

www.ingramcontent.com/pod-product-compliance
Lightning Source LLC
Chambersburg PA
CBHW061230150426
42812CB00054BA/2555